Edexcel GCSE

History Controlled Assessment

CA6 Government and protest in the USA 1945–70

Cathy Warren, Rob Bircher,
Daniel Magnoff and Jane Shuter
Series editor: Angela Leonard

In memory of David Wilkinson, whose passion for history was an inspiration.

A PEARSON COMPANY

Introduction

This unit is about how and why people in the USA campaigned and protested about important issues affecting their lives between 1945 and 1970. It also considers how American governments responded to these demands.

One of the most important developments in this period was that black people organised a range of protests to try to gain equality under the laws. This is known as the civil rights movement. There were different campaigns in various places and each had its own focus. There was not just one civil rights movement but various different organisations and leaders. By the end of the 1960s, progress had been made but there were still many social and economic problems for black Americans, who continued to face racial discrimination and prejudice.

The 1960s also witnessed protests by other groups. Many people protested against the war in Vietnam and feminists campaigned for women's rights. You will see how different forms of protest affected the way America viewed itself. Peaceful protests sometimes met with a violent response. This affected public opinion and helped to put pressure on the government. Yet some people became dissatisfied with this strategy of non-violence and turned instead towards violent protest.
This created a climate of fear and uncertainty, which in turn was heightened by the assassination of leading individuals, such as President John F. Kennedy and the campaigners Malcolm X and Martin Luther King.

Part A of this book covers:

- the civil rights movement 1945–62

- changes in the civil rights movement 1963–70

- the presidency – Eisenhower, Kennedy and Johnson

- protest and dissent – mass protest and assassination as factors for change 1955–70.

For your controlled assessment in this unit, you will learn how to carry out an enquiry (Part A) and how to analyse and evaluate representations of history (Part B). Later sections of this book cover the skills you will need to be successful in unit 4.

Your Part A enquiry will focus in detail on one key question. In Part B you will focus on representations of history: how to analyse, compare and evaluate different views of the impact of protest movements and the responses of government.

Contents

Government and protest in the USA 1945–70

Part A Carry out a historical enquiry

A1 The civil rights movement 1945–62

> ### Learning outcomes
>
> By the end of this topic, you should be able to:
>
> * explain some of the forces driving change and resisting change for civil rights
> * explain the development of methods of protest in the civil rights movement
> * explain why some methods of protest worked better than others.

The movement and change

The **civil rights** movement in the USA aimed to end discrimination against black Americans. Civil rights are the rights that citizens of a country have by law. All American citizens had equal rights according to the law: regardless of whether they were black or white. But in many states of the USA, black people were not allowed this equality. Here there was massive opposition to black people having the same rights as white people.

The civil rights movement was a long and difficult struggle against this opposition. The story of the civil rights movement has many twists and turns as those involved in it tried different ways to get the rights they had by law.

> **Civil rights:** the rights that citizens of a country have by law.

'Engines of change' and roadblocks

Changes take place in history for a range of different reasons. The driving forces behind these changes are sometimes called 'engines of change'. They are the things which cause changes to occur.

They are like the engine of a bus, driving groups of people along a road. Then there are things that oppose this change: maybe stopping it or making it take a different route. We can think of these as being like roadblocks for our bus of change.

There were several different forces causing changes and blocking changes in the civil rights movement. Three of the most important are (a) government action (b) social forces and (c) organisations and individuals.

Government action

The USA has two different levels of government. There is a **federal** government which sets laws for all the states of the United States together. Then each state has its own government and its own laws.

At the start of our period 1945–62, officially, everyone born in the USA was a US citizen and all citizens had the right to vote. But the real situation was quite different. Some states had legal **segregation**. The argument of these so-called 'Jim Crow' laws was that black and white citizens could both have the same rights, but to separate things. Both could have the same right to educate their children, for example, but not in the same schools.

Federal: the United States is a collection of different states all bound together into a federation, with a federal government and federal laws.

Segregation: keeping separate.

NAACP: the National Association for the Advancement of Colored People. It began in 1909.

Ku Klux Klan: a racist white group.

Social forces

Many different social changes had an impact on the civil rights movement. The Second World War, at the start of the period you are studying, is a great example. The USA played a major part in defeating the forces of racism and persecution. Over 1.2 million black men joined up to fight the Nazis, fighting for freedoms that they did not have themselves. Many were determined to continue the fight when they got home.

Source A: A former corporal from Alabama explains how the war has affected him.

> I spent four years in the army to free a bunch of Dutchmen and Frenchmen and I'm hanged if I'm going to let the Alabama version of the Germans kick me around when I get home.

But as well as social changes that pushed the movement forward, there were social attitudes that stood in its way. Racism was very deeply ingrained in much of America, not just in the South. Many white people could not begin to imagine their black neighbours as being equals. They believed black people were naturally inferior – not to be trusted with responsibility or authority. Perhaps behind much racism was also fear – what would life be like for white people if black people were in charge?

Organisations and individuals

Organisations like the **NAACP** campaigned against segregation. When successful, these campaigns could take the movement closer to its goals. But organisations like the **Ku Klux Klan** had enormous influence too: focusing white people's racist attitudes and fears and using violence and murder to intimidate black people. Individuals also had an impact on the history of the civil rights movement – both in inspiring protest and in blocking change.

Activities

1. As you work through this chapter, complete a chart like the one started here that identifies things that drove change and things that blocked it or slowed it down. One example has been added to get you started.

Factor	How it drove change or blocked change
Second World War	Black Americans fought for freedom in Europe and Asia and were determined to fight for it at home as well.

2. Think about ways in which you would fight for your rights as a citizen. What rights would you fight for and how would you fight for them?

3. Research the Ku Klux Klan to find out how they acted to block the civil rights movement. Use reliable textbooks rather than web research to get started.

Segregation and voting rights

Two main ways in which black Americans were denied their civil rights were segregation and not being allowed to vote.

Segregation was based on the idea that black people and white people could have separate access to services: so as we saw on page 4, each could have access to education, just not the same schools. As long as the services were equally good, no one's civil rights would suffer. The problem with this, though, was that the services were not equally good. Black schools, for example, were given very little money compared to white schools. White children were therefore much better educated. Black Americans were not being treated equally: in fact they were being treated unfairly in almost every way imaginable.

Voting rights were rigged too. All US citizens had the right to vote, according to federal law. But local laws in some states put up obstacles to stop black people voting. For example, some states required voters to be able to show that their grandfather had been allowed to vote too: not likely if your grandfather had been black. Or voters had to complete a literacy test, with black voters being given much harder tests or simply being told they had failed. And then there was the threat of violence against black people who tried to vote.

Living in a segregated society was deeply unfair. Being prevented from voting meant black people had no chance of influencing politicians to get rid of segregation.

Follow up your enquiry

Research the different ways in which segregation affected black people's lives in the 1950s and 1960s. You could focus on two or three of these areas:

- education
- transportation
- leisure activities
- employment
- housing.

Activities

4. Write a diary entry, imagining you are a black teenager living in a segregated town. Describe how you feel about the way you live, and what you would like to do that you can't.

5. Why do you think black people stayed in the segregated states? Why not just move to other states?

Using the law

The USA is a democracy where all people are supposed to have equal rights in law. This meant the civil rights movement could use the legal system to protest against inequality and segregation.

Brown v. Board of Education of Topeka

Because there were so many cases where segregation meant federal law about equal rights was being broken, one protest route was to take these cases to court. The NAACP (see page 5) used lawyers to keep pressing rulings against segregation. Often the lawyers were volunteers who wanted to aid the civil rights movement. But the process was a long and difficult one. It was not until 1954 that the NAACP managed to take a case through all the stages to obtain a victory that applied to all public (state) schools in the USA: *Brown v. Topeka*.

Oliver Brown was a black parent who objected to the fact that his eight-year-old daughter, Linda, was denied entry to a nearby all-white school. Instead she had to travel to an all-black school over a mile away. This case was supported by several other examples from across the country.

The leading lawyer for the NAACP was Thurgood Marshall. He argued that black children had the same abilities as white children but were hampered by segregated schools. He used expert witnesses and social science research to support his arguments.

ResultsPlus
Top Tip

In your study of protests, don't assume that a change in the law did actually change people's lives. Think about the factors which could hold up change.

Source B: The Brown family, Topeka, Kansas, 1954. Linda is on the left.

In order to win the case, Marshall needed to convince a majority of the nine Supreme Court judges. It looked as if Marshall might fail, not least because of the reluctant attitude of Chief Justice Vinson. The case was due to be re-argued for the final time when Vinson died. The new Chief Justice was Earl Warren, who surprised almost everyone – including President Dwight Eisenhower, who had appointed him – by giving wholehearted support to desegregation (see page 28).

Source C: Chief Justice Warren delivers the unanimous Supreme Court ruling on the *Brown* case, 17 May 1954.

Does segregation of children in public schools solely on the basis of race… deprive the children…of equal educational opportunities? We believe that it does. To separate…solely because of their race generates a feeling of inferiority…unlikely ever to be undone… We conclude that in the field of public education the doctrine of 'separate but equal' has no place. Separate educational facilities are inherently unequal.

A major block – Southern resistance

The *Brown* verdict was a milestone for civil rights: it showed that the legal route could get results. On the other hand, there was a big difference between winning a legal case and changing the situation in practice. Some states cooperated, such as Missouri and Kentucky: so-called 'border' states between the South and the North.

In the **Deep South**, though, there was much greater hostility and resistance. White Citizens' Councils were set up to defend the practice of segregation. Senator Harry Byrd called for 'massive resistance', and 101 congressmen signed a 'Southern Manifesto' expressing their resentment at federal government's meddling with their state law and their determination to resist desegregation.

Opposition to desegregation and to **integration** was highly effective in the South. Rules were twisted to ensure that black students were not allowed into white schools. Laws to make sure all children went to school were suspended. This was a way of making sure that black children didn't go to school. Teachers of mixed classes had their teaching licences taken away. Sometimes financial aid was removed from integrated schools or grants were given to white children to attend private white-only schools. If all else failed to prevent integration, schools were closed.

Deep South: the states at the Southern edge of the USA: Alabama, Georgia, Louisiana, Mississippi and South Carolina in particular. These states had been highly dependent on black slave labour for their plantation agriculture before the Civil War (1861–1865).

Integration: the opposite of segregation; also meaning black Americans having the same opportunities as white Americans, not just the right to access the same services.

Activities

6. What do you think was most important in getting the *Brown v. Topeka* victory:
    * the role of a key individual(s)?
    * the organisation of the NAACP?
    * right timing/it had to happen eventually?
    * something else?

    Give reasons for your answers.

7. Compare the methods used to oppose desegregation. Which kinds (if any) were:
    * legal protests?
    * semi-legal?
    * illegal?

Case study: the law and Little Rock

States in the Deep South, such as Georgia and Mississippi, made it clear that integration would be strongly opposed. The situation was slightly different in Arkansas. Race relations in the capital, Little Rock, were relatively good. It was a small community of just over 100,000 people, and about a quarter of the population was black. Although some facilities were segregated, such as hotels, theatres, restaurants and toilets, there had been significant desegregation, for example for libraries, parks, buses and hospitals. Arkansas was therefore willing to comply with the *Brown* decision, at least in a token fashion.

Rigging the system

The plan for integration in Little Rock was designed to avoid controversy. Two new schools were built: one in the white side of town and one in the black side. But a third school, the all-white Central High School, posed a problem. Integration would have to be permitted because black middle-class parents were bound to want their children to go there.

The authorities rigged the system to make it unlikely that black students would get in. Students had to meet rigged standards like 'character' and 'health' to get in. These criteria whittled down the black applicants from 75 to 25 children. Then the authorities did all they could to convince the remaining families not to continue with their application.

Source D: Elizabeth Eckford leaves Central High School, Little Rock, having been turned away, on 4 September 1957.

The Little Rock Nine

Only nine students were brave enough to continue to try to attend the school. They became famous as the 'Little Rock Nine' and one of their number, Elizabeth Eckford, became a symbol for the civil rights movement.

Source E: Elizabeth Eckford's recollection of the events of 4 September 1957.

> I walked up to the guard who had let the white students in …When I tried to squeeze past him, he raised his bayonet and then the other guards moved in and raised their bayonets …I was very frightened and didn't know what to do. I turned around and the crowd came toward me …Somebody started yelling, 'Lynch her! Lynch her!' I tried to see a friendly face somewhere in the mob … I looked into the face of an old woman and it seemed a kind face, but when I looked at her again, she spat on me. They came closer, shouting, 'No nigger bitch is going to get in our school'.

Eckford managed to escape because she was helped by two white people, a *New York Times* reporter and a member of the local NAACP.

Opposition from Governor Faubus

The guards who prevented the 'Little Rock Nine' from entering Central High were acting on the orders of Orval Faubus, the governor of Arkansas. In times of emergency the governor had the authority to call out the National Guard – local volunteers who had received military training. Faubus had been spreading rumours that black troublemakers were buying weapons. He appeared on local television, predicting blood on the streets if integration continued. By trying to stop educational integration Faubus was hoping to gain popularity with white voters – at almost any cost.

Repeated rulings by the Federal District Court forced Faubus to remove the National Guard, but he simply replaced them with police whom he then encouraged to turn a blind eye to threats and violence from white protestors.

When the school reopened on 23 September, the 'Little Rock Nine' did get in, but only after the police rescued them from enraged protestors.

The media and President Eisenhower

Public opinion in America and the wider world was influenced by reports about Little Rock using onsite TV cameras. This was a relatively new development in the media. Some of the most shocking reports included interviews with innocent-looking white girls, who expressed violently racist views. President Eisenhower realised how damaging the crisis was becoming and therefore appeared on national television, announcing his decision to use federal troops to restore order. He sent 1,000 paratroopers and placed the Arkansas National Guard under federal control.

Source F: President Eisenhower's televised address, 24 September 1957.

> Mob rule cannot be allowed to override the decisions of our courts… At a time when we face grave situations abroad because of the hatred that Communism bears toward a system of government based on human rights, it would be difficult to exaggerate the harm that is being done… Our enemies are gloating over this incident…We are portrayed as a violator of those standards…which the peoples of the world united to proclaim in the Charter of the United Nations.

Success at Central High?

Despite the president finally giving strong support to integration at Central High, it would be mistaken to regard Little Rock as a clear-cut victory for civil rights. Although the black students were eventually allowed into Central High, their daily experiences were very unpleasant: they were repeatedly victimised and abused, even while the federal troops were present. The situation worsened after November 1957, when the National Guard took over once more.

Only one black student, Ernest Green, succeeded in graduating before Governor Faubus closed all public schools in Little Rock in 1958. Only three black students dared to enrol when Central High reopened the following year, and by 1964 just 123 out of about 7,000 black students attended desegregated schools in Little Rock. Widespread integration did not take place until the 1970s. The crisis at Little Rock in 1957 therefore revealed the scale of the problems that the civil rights movement needed to overcome.

Source G: This is a photo of a rally held in Little Rock against Central High's integration (January 1959).

Activities

8. Would you use Little Rock as a case study to show:
   - a big step forward for the civil rights movement?
   - an example of the difficulties the movement faced?
   - an example of the successful use of the law?
   - an example of the tension between federal and state government?

   Give reasons for and against each option.

9. What do you think motivated each of these key individuals at Little Rock:
   - President Eisenhower?
   - Governor Faubus?
   - Elizabeth Eckford?

10. Study Source G. Why were these people so strongly against black children going to Central High?

11. Explain why the media could be useful to the civil rights movement.

12. Was Little Rock more of a failure than a success for civil rights? Draw up two lists headed Success and Failure to help you answer this question.

The Montgomery Bus Boycott – a turning point?

Limitations of the legal route

Using the law as a lever for change produced results with *Brown v. Topeka*, although Little Rock showed the limitations of the legal route:

- where state government and the white population were strongly against integration, it was almost impossible to make changes through the courts alone
- federal government gave only weak support for integration because of fears that white voters would turn against the president.

Changing the law was not forcing actual changes in black people's lives. To be effective, other forms of protest were needed too. One of the most effective was the boycott.

Did you know?

We use two Latin terms to describe situations where what the law says doesn't match what is actually happening:

de jure describes the position according to the law

de facto describes what was actually happening in practice.

Boycotts and economic protests

A boycott is when a large group of people refuses to do something, in order to protest. It works best in economic situations: especially when the regular customers of a service stop using that service. You can see that a boycott wouldn't work very well with a school – people didn't want the black children turning up anyway. But the bus boycott of 1955–56 in Montgomery, Alabama, was a different scenario, as we shall now see.

Rosa Parks refuses to move

The rules for segregation on Montgomery buses were a longstanding cause of complaint. The rear seats were for black people only, and the ones towards the front were reserved for white people. There was a middle-zone in which black people might sit, providing no white person was sitting in this row. On 1 December 1955 a woman called

Rosa Parks was told to stand because a white passenger wanted one seat in this row. She refused to move and was arrested.

Boycott

In response to her arrest, an organisation – the Montgomery Improvement Association – was set up and a preacher, Martin Luther King, agreed to lead it. The first tactic was a one-day boycott of all Montgomery buses for these demands:

- bus drivers to treat black passengers courteously
- seating to be on a first-come, first-served basis (with black passengers filling the bus from the rear and white passengers from the front)
- black bus drivers for black routes.

These moderate demands met with an extreme response. Black people who joined the boycott were threatened with losing their jobs and sometimes by direct violence. The leaders of the boycott were arrested in an attempt to intimidate them. The effect was simply to increase the determination of the protestors. Complete desegregation became their objective and the boycott was maintained for 381 days.

Legal success

Alongside the boycott, the NAACP also took the case to court and gained this ruling:

Source H: The verdict of the Alabama Middle District Court in *Browder v. Gayle*, November 1956.

> The enforced segregation of Negro and white passengers on motor buses operating in the city of Montgomery violates the Constitution and laws of the United States…denies and deprives plaintiffs and other Negro citizens…of the equal protection of the laws and due process of law.

Montgomery's mayor appealed against this decision, but it was upheld by Chief Justice Warren in the Supreme Court. Black and white passengers could ride together on the buses of Montgomery without segregation.

Roadblock blasted?

The Montgomery Bus Boycott was a turning point in the civil rights movement. Black protestors saw that by acting together they had significant economic power.

During the boycott, the bus company's revenue went down by 65%. Local businesses lost custom. It was estimated that the boycott caused losses of about $1 million. Therefore white businessmen became anxious to resolve the dispute.

Success was also due to solidarity in the black community. People walked together, or shared cars and taxis, to get to work (organisers arranged low taxi rates and car-share pick-up points). They resisted intimidation and tried to avoid violence. Crucially, there wasn't a way of rigging the system: the bus companies needed black passengers.

There were also another two key reasons why the boycott was successful. One was the leadership of Martin Luther King. The other was the way the NAACP organised the protest around the figure of Rosa Parks.

Martin Luther King – ideal leadership?

Martin Luther King

King's eloquence and bravery inspired many black people.

King was an ideal figure for media attention: photogenic, expressed his views skilfully.

His Christian values and commitment to non-violence meant he wasn't seen as a threat by many white Americans.

Activities

13. Compare the Montgomery Bus Boycott with the Little Rock Nine. What factors made Montgomery more successful?

14. When might a boycott be a bad choice of protest (for example, would it have worked against expensive whites-only sports clubs?)

Rosa Parks – the ideal figurehead?

The arrest of Rosa Parks on 1 December 1955 for challenging segregated transport is one of the most famous incidents in the civil rights movement. The Montgomery Bus Boycott is sometimes misleadingly portrayed as a spontaneous protest in support of a woman who had been too tired to surrender her seat after an exhausting day's work. In fact:

Rosa Parks

Rosa Parks had been involved with the NAACP since the early 1940s.

Parks had been involved in several civil rights protests over the years.

She had clashed with this particular bus driver before and had sworn never to ride his bus again.

This wasn't the first bus boycott: there had been one in Louisiana in 1953, which the NAACP used as a template for Montgomery.

The NAACP had nearly organised its boycott after Claudette Colvin, aged 15, was arrested for not moving when told to. But Colvin later became pregnant whilst not married and so was not considered 'reputable'.

Parks was, on the other hand, perfect for the media: she was very respectable, a Christian and a valued member of the community.

None of this is to take away from Rosa Parks' bravery and her achievement, but it is important to see that in choosing to go with her, the NAACP was thinking of media publicity as being as crucial for the success of the protest as the economic impact was. The events of 1 December 1954 provided an ideal opportunity for action.

Building on the boycott

The success of the Montgomery Bus Boycott gave the civil rights movement a major boost. In some ways the boycott marks the point where the movement really got going. It could make a real impact as long as its targets were well chosen and the protestors stayed strong against the opposition. The leadership of the protests was very important too. So it set out a blueprint for future protests – but could they be as successful?

Training protestors

The Bus Boycott established King as one of the most important leaders of the civil rights movement. He set up his own organisation in 1957: the Southern Christian Leadership Conference (**SCLC**). This started to train people in effective non-violent protest. Citizenship Schools were designed to teach black citizens how to pass the voter registration tests (see page 6) as well as teaching about civil rights, democracy and non-violent protest.

This training programme was deeply unpopular with white opposition and schools were closed down and teachers had their licences taken away. But the schools started up again elsewhere, using volunteer teachers.

There was also opposition, however, from within the black community. King wanted black churches to join with the SCLC to give it support and get church members educated. But many churches believed King was pushing the movement away from the legal route, the safest and most acceptable form of protest – even if it was the slowest.

At the same time, King was also criticised by other black activists for not going far or fast enough.

> **SCLC:** the Southern Christian Leadership Conference. It began in 1957.
>
> **SNCC:** the Student Non-Violent Coordinating Committee. It began in 1960.
>
> **CORE:** the Congress of Racial Equality. It began in 1942.
>
> **Sit-in:** a non-violent type of protest in which protestors sit down in an area and refuse to move.

Student power and sit-ins

After the success of Montgomery, large numbers of students, both black and white, joined in the civil rights protests. They wanted change to happen fast. A new organisation was created: the Student Non-Violent Coordinating Committee (**SNCC**). This youth movement was inspired by experienced activists from the Congress of Racial Equality (**CORE**), such as James Farmer. The SNCC organised a new kind of non-violent economic protest: **sit-ins**.

On 1 February 1960 four students seated themselves at the 'white-only' section of the lunch counter of the downtown branch of Woolworths in Greensboro, North Carolina. They were not expecting to be served but refused to move to the 'colored' section. They sat in the 'white' section until closing time, and returned the following day with 23 other students, who continued the sit-in. By the end of the third day over 80 students were involved.

Similar protests spread into other Southern states. By April around 2,000 protestors had been arrested.

In order to make even greater impact the protestors adopted the tactic of 'Jail not bail' (bail is a pledge of money made to ensure someone accused of a crime turns up to their trial). If protestors refused bail, the court would have to keep them in jail until their trial. The protestors wanted to overwhelm the jails and make the system unworkable.

The sit-in movement affected over 200 cities in 20 states, scoring some spectacular successes. Woolworths lost 20% of its business and agreed to desegregate its lunch counters. By 1961 more than 120 Southern communities had some desegregated eating facilities. The success led to 'wade-ins' at segregated swimming pools, and 'kneel-ins' at segregated churches.

Activities

15. What are the similarities between sit-ins and the bus boycotts?
16. Why didn't protestors use sit-ins against the many restaurants that refused to serve black customers at all? (Hint: Woolworths had a lot of black customers.)

Freedom Riders – a direct challenge

At the same time, CORE planned an ambitious challenge to segregation. Black and white protestors, known as '**Freedom Riders**', bought tickets in a non-segregated state and travelled into the danger zones of the South, refusing to obey segregation laws. A recent Supreme Court ruling had confirmed that segregation was illegal on interstate transport. But CORE knew that this protest method would guarantee an extreme reaction in the Deep South. They wanted to provoke this reaction, and they wanted the TV cameras to film it.

Source I: Recollections by the CORE leader, James Farmer.

> We planned the Freedom Ride with the intention of creating a crisis. We were counting on the racists of the South to do our work for us. We figured the government would have to respond if we created a situation that was headline news all over the world.

Freedom Riders: a federal law meant interstate buses should not be segregated. Civil rights protestors, known as 'Freedom Riders' rode on these buses into segregated states to show that the law was often not being obeyed.

The tactic worked. In Anniston, the police allowed the local Ku Klux Klan to firebomb a bus (see Source J). In Birmingham, the police chief gave his officers the day off, allowing racist mobs a free hand. In Montgomery, Freedom Riders were beaten with baseball bats while the police refused to intervene.

Source J: Freedom Riders watch as the bus they were travelling in goes up in flames after being bombed in Anniston, 14 May 1961.

The president and progress

The new president in January 1961, John F. Kennedy, had to decide how far to use federal forces to prevent further violence. The president had no choice but to force through the desegregation of interstate travel. Segregation signs were removed and instead all interstate travel companies had to display signs stating that seating was provided 'without regard to race, colour, creed, or national origin'.

Activity

17. Look back over the chart you have completed for this chapter (Activity 1 on page 5).
    - Which were the most important factors driving the civil rights movement?
    - Which were the biggest obstacles to the movement gaining ground?

Your conclusion so far

From this topic, we have seen:
- NAACP success in the Brown case showed that the law could back integration.
- Effective forms of protest developed with strong leadership, organisation and support.
- The strong backlash from Southern whites seriously limited progress.
- The president had a key role in securing progress in civil rights.

From what you have learned in this topic, to what extent do you think non-violent protest, the media and the government were all interconnected?

To answer this question, consider:
- would non-violent protest have worked without the media?
- would the president have acted differently if the media had reported violent protest?
- how would the media have reacted to black people using violent protest?

A2 Changes in the civil rights movement 1963–70

Learning outcomes

By the end of this topic, you should be able to:

- describe differences in the civil rights movement before and after 1963
- identify how government actions affected civil rights protests
- explain why civil rights protests changed.

Changing times

In the 1960s, non-violent protests and the publicity surrounding them increased. One of the ways that non-violent **direct action** was supposed to work was to put pressure on **segregationists** to change by getting them to show themselves in a bad light in the media. This pressure produced an increasingly violent reaction from opponents of the movement. Worldwide media coverage of this violence put pressure on the federal government to act.

1. Federal government does nothing to smooth the road or remove the roadblock.

2. Federal government smoothes the road...

3. Federal government smoothes the road and removes roadblock...

4. Federal government smoothes the road – but is the road still going in the right direction?

5. Change the bus to something that doesn't need the government's road and can remove roadblocks itself?

In this way, non-violent protests scored some major victories, as we have seen. Changes in federal law forced an end to segregation and started to tackle discrimination. But changes in the federal law did not always mean changes in everyday life. During the 1960s, a growing number of black people began to agree that integration was too slow in coming and, when it came, did not produce equality. Were the sacrifices of those getting beaten up, imprisoned and murdered really worth it?

More and more people began to believe that peaceful protest was not getting anywhere fast enough. Some of them began to support more radical action. Other civil rights campaigners, including Martin Luther King, continued to protest by non-violent direct action.

Direct action: doing something directly to try to make changes, e.g. demonstrations, boycotts, sit-ins. Indirect action would include using your vote to change a situation you don't like.

Segregationists: supporters of the belief that black and white people should have separate facilities.

Activities

1. Which of the five scenarios shown opposite do you think best describes the relationship between the federal government and the civil rights movement in the 1960s?

2. Explain why some people thought the federal government should not do anything for civil rights.

3. Explain why some people thought the federal government should do a lot more than it had done for civil rights.

4. What do you think the federal government wanted to achieve with civil rights changes? Was it the same as what the civil rights movement wanted?

5. Explain why some people might have got frustrated with non-violent protest and wanted to use more radical methods.

Non-violence meets increased violence

Non-violent protests continued to get massive media attention and achieve big successes in forcing integration, but they were met with more and more violence from segregationists.

Birmingham, Alabama

In 1963, civil rights campaigners targeted Birmingham, Alabama for a full-scale, non-violent desegregation campaign. Birmingham was an ideal choice for a showcase of non-violence against racist hate:

- the city had not carried out a single piece of desegregation
- it was nicknamed 'Bombingham' because black houses, churches and businesses were blown up so often
- its chief of police, 'Bull' Connor, was said to have given the Ku Klux Klan 15 minutes to beat up the Freedom Riders of 1961 before his police moved in to halt the violence.

The campaign began on 3 April with anti-segregation marches. So many adults were jailed that one of the organisers, James Bevel, began to train high school children in protest tactics, to make sure that the demonstrations continued. The first big children's demonstration was on 2 May. By the end of the day, about 1,000 young people had been arrested. The next day, more young people marched. This time, dogs and firehoses were used. There were many more arrests – Martin Luther King included. The stories and photos of Birmingham were published worldwide. President Kennedy said he felt ashamed when he saw the photo shown in Source A on page 16.

This worldwide media coverage put huge pressure on the city. The mayor and protest leaders met on 10 May to work out how to break down segregation in the city. The governor of Alabama tried to disrupt the talks by sending in state troops; violence flared up. But President Kennedy sent in federal troops and calm was restored. The mayor passed desegregation laws and lunch counters and shops desegregated. Black people were able to apply for jobs they had previously been forbidden to apply for. The campaign had worked.

Building on Birmingham

Birmingham was chosen carefully by campaigners as a city guaranteed to generate large scale, violent opposition to the civil rights movement. After the success of the campaign there, President Kennedy made a speech promising 'to ask Congress to act, to make a commitment it has not fully made in this century to the proposition that race has no place in American life or law'. But these were just words – important words, but words just the same. A Civil Rights Bill was under discussion in Congress, but it still made little progress against opposition from the Southern states.

And violent opposition to change was still growing. Groups such as the Ku Klux Klan carried out bombings and murders, including the killing of NAACP leader Medgar Evers in June 1963. Black people felt increasingly threatened by the violence and ignored by government. There were riots in many towns and cities.

The civil rights movement needed to build on Birmingham and continue the pressure on federal government to make big changes. Civil rights groups worked together to organise a march on Washington in August 1963 to convince Congress to act to support civil rights.

- The march on Washington was the biggest civil rights action ever: over 200,000 demonstrators.
- There were about 3,000 reporters and the march was one of the first events to be broadcast live around the world by the newly launched Telstar satellite.
- Martin Luther King made his 'I have a dream' speech, which became instantly famous.

Source A: William Gadsden, who was crossing the road rather than protesting, being set on by one of 'Bull' Connor's police dogs, 3 May 1963. Marches were often held at noon, when people were out over lunchtime.

Freedom Summer

In 1964 the SNCC decided on a new strategy to continue the pressure on Congress. It had been trying for years to raise the number of black people registered to vote in Mississippi: the most racist and segregated state in the United States. Very few black people dared to vote because of violence and intimidation. And then there were all the barriers to voter registration, like the literacy test (see page 6).

The SNCC sent about 1,000 volunteers to help black people in Mississippi pass voter registration tests. But the strategy was designed to have a much bigger impact. The volunteers were mostly Northern, white, college students from well-off families. The campaigners knew that any violence against young white people in Mississippi would get major news coverage. And the volunteers knew this too.

At least six civil rights workers were killed in Mississippi during the summer (see Source B). There were 80 beatings, 35 shooting 'incidents' and over 1,000 arrests. Over 60 black homes, businesses and churches were bombed.

The campaign failed to get many more black people voting in Mississippi. But it certainly succeeded in increasing the pressure on federal government. The deaths of young white students meant the US media really focused attention on civil rights. Many black campaigners rightly felt this was proof that the media cared more about young white lives than young black ones. But the national shame in the USA about what had happened in Mississippi helped federal government overcome Southern opposition to landmark changes in civil rights law.

ResultsPlus
Top Tip

Part A questions are often about change, for example about 'the nature of change, the factors involved in a change, or turning points that really show change in action.

Source B: Poster issued by the Federal Bureau of Investigation. Schwerner, Chaney and Goodman were all SNCC volunteers. Their bodies were found on 4 August. They had all been shot in the head. Chaney had been beaten first – many of his bones were shattered.

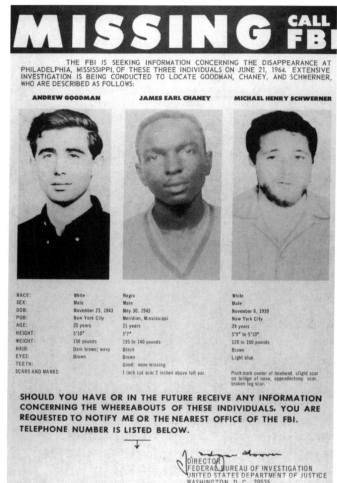

Activities

7. How did the march on Washington's organisers hope it would help the civil rights movement?

8. Do you think Schwerner, Chaney and Goodman died in vain or did their deaths help the movement?

Landmark laws

The role of the federal government

Federal government had to balance the demands of the civil rights movement against the need to get votes from the Southern states.

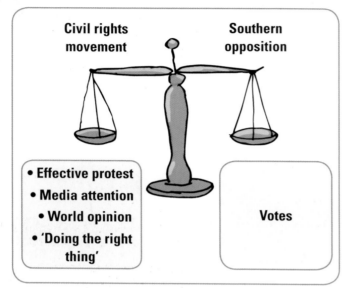

By 1964, the scales had tipped far enough for President Johnson to put his weight behind the Civil Rights Act.

Civil Rights Act

On 2 July 1964, the Civil Rights Act was passed. President Johnson pushed the act through Congress against Southern opposition. The act:

- banned discrimination in education, public places and any business with more than 25 employees
- set up an Equal Employment Opportunity Commission to investigate discrimination
- said that voter registration tests should be the same for black and white people.

Changing law in principle to law in practice

The Civil Rights Act was a huge achievement. But campaigners knew there was a big difference between a law in principle and a law in practice. Although the act officially stopped Southern states giving black people harder registration tests than white people, there was practically nothing to enforce this. Black people needed a fair test for registration and to be protected from violence. The Civil Rights Act had to be enforced.

So civil rights groups protested again for voter registration, beginning in Alabama, at Selma (see page 68), where there had been violent clashes when black people tried to register to vote. State troops attacked protestors and, once again, the USA made world headlines for its abuse of black people.

President Johnson provided an escort of federal troops so the protestors could finish their march to Montgomery and made a speech in which he said 'all of us must overcome the crippling legacy of bigotry and injustice'.

The Voting Rights Act

On 6 August 1965, the Voting Rights Act brought an end to all discriminatory literacy tests for voting. It also set up federal examiners who could go to any state and check that black people were not being discriminated against in voter registration. This stopped states from imposing their own literacy rules or other rules, such as saying that voters must have their own property to be registered to vote.

Source C: From *The Civil Rights Movement,* written by W.T.M. Riches in 1997.

> Julian Bond of SNCC commented in 1968 that, 'the '64 and '65 Acts took the pressure off the country. People weren't as concerned about civil rights because they felt they'd done what they should.' President Johnson wrote in his memoirs: 'With the passing of these Acts the barriers to freedom began tumbling down. At long last the legal rights of American citizens – the right to vote, to have a job, to use public places, to go to school – were given solid protection.'

Activities

9. The Civil Rights Act of 1964 was a huge achievement for the civil rights movement. Draw up a timeline starting in 1945 to show the main events on the road to 1964.

10. Many white people thought the Civil Rights Act should end the protests and violence of the civil rights movement. What arguments do you think these people made for this?

11. President Johnson said 'solid protection' had been given to civil rights: to what extent was that true?

The reasons for civil rights success by 1965

Non-violent protest methods had achieved tremendous success with the Civil Rights Act and the Voting Rights Act. The protest methods had been carefully designed to put maximum pressure on the federal government. Not many protests are as effective as those of the civil rights movement up to 1965. There were various factors involved in this success.

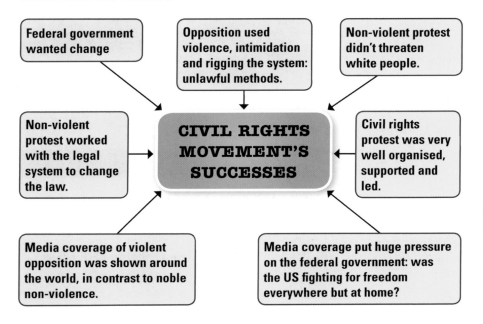

- **Federal government wanted change**
- **Opposition used violence, intimidation and rigging the system: unlawful methods.**
- **Non-violent protest didn't threaten white people.**
- **Non-violent protest worked with the legal system to change the law.**
- **CIVIL RIGHTS MOVEMENT'S SUCCESSES**
- **Civil rights protest was very well organised, supported and led.**
- **Media coverage of violent opposition was shown around the world, in contrast to noble non-violence.**
- **Media coverage put huge pressure on the federal government: was the US fighting for freedom everywhere but at home?**

Protest methods also adapted and built on each other. This list imagines how a civil rights protestor might have seen the links between situations and protest methods:

How protest methods can link up

- bus boycotts were successful
- can't boycott restaurants – but sit-ins work well
- boycotts and sit-ins can't help with improving voting registration: but training and education will
- the opposition is increasing violence against us: encouraging high school kids to join non-violent protests could work against that
- media coverage works best when extreme violence is used against non-violent protestors – engineer flashpoints to focus media attention.

Activities

12. Explain the relationship between the different factors involved in civil rights successes by 1965. Make links between the factors and explain how they worked together to achieve success.

13. Which do you think was most important in achieving the breakthroughs of 1964: protest or government? Explain why.

14. Which of these do you think helped most in achieving the landmark laws of 1964 and 1965? Explain your answer.
    - Little Rock, 1957
    - Montgomery Bus Boycott, 1955
    - Freedom Summer, 1964
    - The March on Washington, 1963
    - *Brown v. Topeka*, 1954.

Riots

From 1965 on, waves of riots swept the USA. Mostly in towns and cities in the North, they were often set off by a particular act of police brutality against black Americans, which is why different cities had riots in different years.

There were major riots in New York (1964), Los Angeles (1965), Chicago and Cleveland (1966), Newark and Detroit (1967), and Washington and Cleveland (1968). There were smaller riots in other towns and cities. There were hundreds of deaths, thousands of arrests and billions of dollars worth of damage. Non-violent actions also fell apart into riots, such as a march for union rights in Memphis, Tennessee, led by Martin Luther King in 1968.

After the great successes of non-violent protest, why did these riots happen?

- Although the landmark acts of 1964 and 1965 promised great changes, states acted quickly to block major changes. The new laws had done nothing to actually enforce change.
- The riots were also a reaction to the long-term problems of city-living for black people – unemployment, overcrowding and poor services.
- Martin Luther King's view that everyone had underestimated both the extent of prejudice in the USA and how much black Americans resented this prejudice.

On 4 April 1968, Martin Luther King was assassinated by a white gunman (see page 36). There were riots in over a hundred American towns and cities over the week that followed. It took over 55,000 soldiers to stop the riots.

Many white people who had previously supported the civil rights movement turned against it. The image of innocent, non-violent black people being persecuted by white police was replaced in their minds with the image of an angry black young man with a petrol bomb.

Source D: This photograph from August 1965 in Watts, Los Angeles, shows how black residents used violence to take control of their poor, crime-ridden neighbourhood.

Activities

15. After all the successes of non-violent protests, explain why the landmark laws of 1964 and 1965 were followed by riots.

16. Imagine you are a white supporter of the civil rights movement who is appalled by the riots of the late 1960s. Write a letter to a civil rights leader explaining why you think violence is not the answer.

Tensions in the civil rights movement

For all its successes and effective organisation of protest, the civil rights movement was never a group of people who all thought the same thing and agreed on the same tactics. There had always been tensions among the different groups and organisations that made up the movement. Broadly speaking, the tensions were about:

- whether non-violent methods were more effective than using violence
- whether white people and black people should work together for racial equality, or whether black people should work alone for their aims
- whether trying to change the law was effective – or whether it didn't actually change anything in everyday life
- whether black people should support integration or not: was integration ever going to result in equality for black people?

This produced a tension within the movement.

Was it possible for black people and white people to live together in harmony and equality?

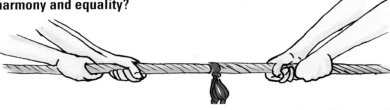

Or should black people accept that white people would never treat them as equals, fight the white system and do what they could for themselves?

One side of this tension is the moderate side (the left side on this diagram). You can see how white people would be less threatened by moderate aims. The other side is radical, and radical aims were likely to make white Americans feel threatened – even those who were supporters of moderate civil rights aims.

Different civil rights organisations supported different aims and methods. Sometimes these changed over time.

National Association for the Advancement of Colored People:
- worked though the courts for legal reform
- aimed for equality for black and white people
- worked with white people to achieve aims.

Southern Christian Leadership Conference:
- dedicated to non-violent protest
- seen as too radical by NAACP
- seen as too moderate by CORE or SNCC.

Student Non-violent Coordinating Committee:
- organised direct-action protests against segregation and for voting rights
- originally supported by fundraising and volunteers in white liberal North
- after 1964 many members felt black people had to defend themselves against violence.

Congress of Racial Equality:
- strong supporters of non-violence (pacifist roots to organisation)
- worked with white supporters on Freedom Rides
- moved towards supporting **black nationalism.**

Black nationalism: the belief that black people should create a black society, independent from white society.

Activities

17. Sort these four organisations into a line going from 'moderate' to 'radical'.

18. Read this list of factors that may have influenced changes in the civil rights movement. Which three do you think were the most significant and why?

   a) assassination of Martin Luther King

   b) disappointment that landmark laws were not being enforced

   c) major problems of poverty and bad housing for black people in US cities

   d) President Johnson felt he had done enough for civil rights

   e) tensions within the civil rights movement

   f) loss of support for the civil rights movement from liberal white people

   g) continuing opposition to black civil rights in the South

   h) resentment about the prejudice faced by black people.

Follow up your enquiry

Research these organisations in more detail. To what extent were they able to work together up to 1964? Why did joint efforts start to fall apart after 1965?

Black Power

Black people still faced discrimination and violence and felt, often rightly, they could not trust the government or the police to protect them – much of the violence against civil rights campaigners came from the police. In June 1966, James Meredith (the first black student at the University of Mississippi in 1962 – see page 30) led a 'March Against Fear' through Mississippi. He was shot on the second day of the march. Martin Luther King took over the march, joined by Stokely Carmichael of SNCC. King's speeches stressed the need to continue non-violent action, but the more militant speeches of Stokely Carmichael, urging people to demand '**Black Power**', gained increasing support.

> **Black Power:** movements that aimed to get more power for black people, to fight against the oppression of black people and to help create a strong black identity.

The Black Panthers

In October 1966, in Oakland, California, Huey Newton and Bobby Seale set up the Black Panther Party. The group had a ten-point plan, but the point that the media paid most attention to was the monitoring of police brutality. Panthers would follow police officers to prevent any abuse of black people by the police (sometimes called 'patrolling the pigs'). Sometimes these situations turned violent and there were deaths on both sides. Many black people came to see the Panthers as a more effective community police than the state police force. The Black Panthers also organised community projects, such as free breakfasts and healthcare in poor black areas. Not surprisingly, the government saw them as a threat, especially as the movement spread. By 1968, there were Black Panther groups in 25 American cities.

Activities

19. To what extent were the aims of the Black Panthers different from those of moderate groups like the NAACP or SCLC?

20. Explain why 'Black Power' alarmed federal government in the USA.

21. Study Source F. Do you think the Black Panthers were more connected to black people's needs than groups working for black voting rights?

Source E: The Black Panthers' ten-point plan of 1966. Point 1 was suggesting a form of separation, but with government funding.

1. We want freedom. We want power to determine the destiny of our black and oppressed communities.
2. We want full employment for our people.
3. We want an end to the robbery by the capitalists of our black and oppressed communities.
4. We want decent housing, fit for the shelter of human beings.
5. We want decent education for our people that exposes the true nature of this decadent American society. We want education that teaches us our true history and our role in the present-day society.
6. We want completely free health care for all black and oppressed people.
7. We want an immediate end to police brutality and murder of black people, other people of color, all oppressed people inside the United States.
8. We want an immediate end to all wars of aggression. [This was against the Vietnam war.]
9. We want freedom for all black and oppressed people now held in U.S. Federal, state, county, city and military prisons and jails. We want trials by a jury of peers for all persons charged with so-called crimes under the laws of this country.
10. We want land, bread, housing, education, clothing, justice, peace and people's community control of modern technology.

Source F: Members of the Black Panther Party stand behind tables ready to distribute free clothing to the public, New Haven, Connecticut, 28 September 1969.

Malcolm X

Malcolm X became the voice of many angry black people who felt non-violent protest had failed.

He started his political life by joining the **Nation of Islam** while in prison. This group believed that attempts at integration had failed and that black people would be better off living separately rather than in a so-called integrated society where they always had the worst living and working conditions. After prison, he changed his name from Malcolm Little to Malcolm X. The X stood for his family's real African name, lost forever during the horrors of the slave trade.

Malcolm X spoke out against non-violent action and criticised leaders such as Martin Luther King. While Martin Luther King wanted to work with white politicians and convince them to work for civil rights, Malcolm X did not. He saw white politicians as the enemy. While Martin Luther King focused on voter registration and desegregation in the South, Malcolm X focused on the inequalities faced by black people everywhere, North and South. While he assured people he was not urging violent revolt, he did urge black people to respond to violence with violence.

> **Nation of Islam:** a religious organisation that began in 1930 with the aim of improving life for black Americans. It borrows some ideas from the Islamic religion but also has some non-Islamic beliefs.

Activities

22. Compare the influence of Martin Luther King and Malcolm X on the way black Americans protested for civil rights.

23. Many civil rights campaigners criticised Malcolm X very strongly. What do you think their criticisms were about?

Martin Luther King

- Christian preacher
- Worked to end segregation and for racial equality
- Believed in black people and white people working together for equality
- Believed non-violent direct action was the best way to achieve progress
- Believed working with the system would deliver the best results
- Focused on ending segregation and voting restrictions on black Americans: less successful when tackling urban poverty
- Was a huge influence on the civil rights movement
- Assassinated in 1968

Malcolm X

- Muslim, onetime member of Nation of Islam
- Criticised white America for persecution of black people
- Said black people should live completely separately from the white system (changed these views later in life)
- Believed black people were better than white people
- Believed black Americans should defend themselves against violence 'by any means necessary'
- Criticised those who worked with the white system to try to improve black civil rights
- Focused on the poverty and exploitation black people suffered in US cities
- Was a huge influence on the Black Power movement
- Assassinated in 1965

Changes in the civil rights movement 1963–70: what had changed?

Your course makes a division between the civil rights movement from 1945 to 1962, and 1963 to 1970. This chapter has tried to show some of the ways the movement did change, for example:

- from non-violence to self-defence
- from aiming for equality to aiming for black people controlling their own communities
- from concentrating on integration and equal voting rights to combating black exploitation and poverty
- from changing the law to directly helping the black community.

Of course, the change wasn't as clear cut as that in reality. The struggle for equality went on alongside Black Power movements, organisations changed their stance on issues backwards and forwards, and Black Power and the struggle for legal change worked together as well as against each other. For example, one of the great achievements of Black Power was to make black people feel good about themselves, after so many centuries of slavery, exploitation and prejudice. Americans who were proud to be black made outstanding contributions in all areas of life, including law and government.

The problems of the North

Geography is also important: the South and the North had different problems. In the South, black people suffered from segregation and deliberate, open inequality. They faced blatant, undisguised racism and prejudice. The civil rights movement pressurised federal government to tackle this shameful situation.

But in the North the problems were different. White people and black people usually lived apart, not because of any law but because black people couldn't afford to live anywhere but the poorest city districts. It wasn't something that a change in the law could fix. This needed massive amounts of money. But if states put all their money into improving conditions for black people, it would hurt everyone else. There were no votes in that for the politicians.

Also, there were other changes in society that affected the movement. The Vietnam War became increasingly unpopular in the USA during the later 1960s and early 1970s. To an extent, there was a change in the focus of protest from civil rights to Vietnam. People also got tired of protest and unrest. Many people in the USA reacted by voting for politicians who would look after them and their interests rather than for people with big plans for making America a better place for everyone.

Follow up your enquiry

Review the best internet sites for African American history (your teacher can help you with the sites to go to). Check their coverage of how and why the civil rights movement changed from 1945–62 and 1963–70. What points do they generally agree on? What areas do they differ on?

ResultsPlus
Watch out

Remember not to assume that the amount of progress was the same all over the USA. The problems in the North were harder to tackle.

Your conclusion so far

From this topic we have seen that:

- Pressure from non-violent protest eventually resulted in landmark civil rights laws.
- However, the lack of enforcement of these laws created frustration.
- Black people were also facing serious poverty and prejudice in cities all over America. It was difficult for the movement to tackle these problems.

In November 2008, Barack Obama became the first black president of the United States. From what you have learned in this topic:

- what do you think Martin Luther King would have said about Obama becoming president?
- what do you think Malcolm X would have said about Obama becoming president?

A3 The presidency – Eisenhower, Kennedy and Johnson

> **Learning outcomes**
>
> By the end of this topic, you should be able to:
>
> - describe key features of the presidencies of Eisenhower, Kennedy and Johnson
> - explain their attitudes to the civil rights protests
> - make judgements about the contribution of each president toward the promotion of civil rights.

The president and the federal government

As you have seen in the last two chapters, the civil rights movement protests targeted the federal government. Civil rights campaigners hoped that the federal government would act against individual state governments to end segregation and bring in equality.

Federal government has three parts:

- the president
- Congress
- the Supreme Court.

Starting at the end of the list, the Supreme Court is the top law court in the USA. It played a key role in civil rights when it made rulings against state law. For example, the Supreme Court ruled that segregated schools were against the US Constitution and should be ended (see pages 6–7).

The president nominates the judges of the Supreme Court and the nominees are appointed with the 'advice and consent' of the Senate. Presidents could choose to nominate justices who opposed or supported segregation. These justices were appointed for life so they didn't need to worry about getting re-elected. That meant it was hard to influence them, and so a supreme court justice could go on opposing or promoting a cause for many, many years.

Congress is like the UK's Parliament: it approves new laws. There are two main political parties in the USA – the Republican Party and the Democratic Party. From 1945 up to the end of the 1960s Congress was controlled by the Democrats. The most traditional, anti-integration Southern states voted Democrat too. Republicans in Congress would not vote in favour of civil rights issues so they, together, with the Southern Democrats, formed the 'blocking majority' or the 'Deadlock of Democracy' against civil rights causes.

So, if a president was a Democrat, as both Kennedy and Johnson were, then they needed to keep their party happy. But it also meant that any president, Democrat or Republican, faced powerful opposition right in the heart of federal government.

A political balancing act

The role of the president was very important in the relationship between protest and government over civil rights. The president was at the sharp end of the pressure that protestors and the media put on federal government. But the president was also always under pressure from those who didn't want change: especially, in the case of civil rights, senators from Southern states.

So the president had to perform a political balancing act – he might have a strong idea of where he wanted to go, but whether he got there or not depended on whether he could keep his balance!

Three presidents: Eisenhower, Kennedy and Johnson

Dwight D. Eisenhower

This photo of President Eisenhower shows him in military uniform. His military achievements in the Second World War also brought him to power as president.

President: 1953–61 (served two terms)
Party: Republican
Nickname: 'Ike'

Background

A genuine war hero. During the Second World War, he oversaw the D-Day landings, the liberation of France, and the defeat of Nazi Germany. He was passionately anti-communist.

Politics

Republican. He believed that the government should not interfere too much in people's lives – and federal government should not interfere with state government, either, unless absolutely necessary.

Attitude to civil rights movement

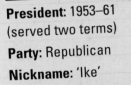

Complicated. He did not believe that federal government should ever force change on people, and he had no wish to upset his backers in the South. But he did appoint Earl Warren as Chief Justice of the Supreme Court, and Warren then acted as a champion of black civil rights. Then the civil rights movement's tactics forced Eisenhower to send federal troops to Little Rock.

Verdict

Oversaw significant civil rights progress, despite his reluctance to get involved.

John F. Kennedy

This unusual picture is the White House's official portrait of Kennedy, painted after his death. It reflects the sadness and confusion that gripped the USA when he was assassinated.

President: 1961–63 (assassinated during first term)
Party: Democrat
Nickname: 'JFK'

Background

Kennedy came from a rich and powerful political family. Looking after the interests of his family was always a high priority.

Politics

Democrat. He promised to use federal government powers to improve everyone's lives in America. However, as president he spent most of his time dealing with international events.

Attitude to civil rights movement

Opportunistic – he supported it when it suited him. Kennedy had only won the election to be president by a tiny majority. He had to keep the support of the Southern Democrats in Congress if he wanted to achieve anything as president.

While Kennedy did lend support to some civil rights actions from the start of his presidency, it was only after the civil rights movement's tactics in Birmingham (1963) forced him to that he really acted to back civil rights.

Verdict

Promised big changes, but couldn't really afford to rock the boat.

Lyndon B. Johnson

After JFK had been assassinated, his vice-president, Johnson, became president. This photo shows Johnson taking the oath of office just after Kennedy's death was announced.

President: 1963–69 (decided not to run for president again after one-and-a-half terms)

Party: Democrat

Nickname: 'LBJ'

Background
Johnson became president when the assassination of Kennedy in 1963 resulted in an automatic promotion of the vice-president. The nation was in mourning for the loss of Kennedy and wanted Johnson to succeed. Therefore, the best strategy for Johnson was to portray himself as someone who would complete Kennedy's policies.

Politics
Democrat. Johnson declared a 'war on poverty' and succeeded in pushing through new laws that he hoped would bring about a 'Great Society'. His programmes relied on large-scale government funding, a booming economy and public support. Unfortunately for Johnson, he also had the Vietnam War to deal with at the same time (see pages 41–42).

Attitude to civil rights movement
Champion. He was able to push through the landmark laws of 1964 and 1965 on the wave of public grief over JFK's death. His 'war on poverty' supported black communities in US cities. And all this as a president who actually came from a Southern state: Texas. But his presidency also saw the rise of Black Power and riots in US cities, along with massive protests against the Vietnam War, and also protests in support of women's rights (see pages 38–40).

Verdict
Was committed to tackling inequality but was limited in what he could achieve because of the powerful social changes sweeping through America.

Follow up your enquiry

Set up your own files on each of the three presidents and build up research notes on each one.

- Remember to keep your focus on the relationship between each president and protests over civil rights. (With Johnson you can consider protests about women's rights and against the Vietnam War as well.)
- Make sure you keep in mind the political tightrope each president had to walk between protestors and the Southern Democrats – record examples of this happening when you find them.

Eisenhower: government and protest

Eisenhower thought the federal government should interfere as little as possible in people's lives. Instead, he thought people should be trusted to do the right thing for the country. So:

- he supported the idea that individual states should have some independence from federal government
- he criticised any group that seemed to act for itself rather than for the good of the country as a whole.

This sort of policy had a big impact on how Eisenhower viewed the civil rights movement. He:

- did not believe that federal government should step in and force people to behave differently
- did not think federal government should set up big projects to improve social conditions
- depended on the Southern states and upheld their right to set some of their own laws and have some independence from federal government
- was not in favour of civil rights groups because he believed they did not act for the good of the country as a whole.

Eisenhower believed changes in society could only be achieved by the will of the majority of people and then only gradually, over a long period of time.

Activities

1. Eisenhower was very worried about the spread of communism around the world. He called the USA the 'land of the free'. What might civil rights campaigners have said about this?

2. Eisenhower, a Republican, was faced by a Democratic majority in Congress for all but two of his eight years as president, so he relied on conservative Democrats to join with his own Republicans to govern effectively. How do you think this affected his attitude to the civil rights movement?

The *Brown v. Topeka* decision

Yet despite all of this, the civil rights movement achieved its biggest success for more than 50 years during the Eisenhower presidency. How did that happen?

Source A: Eisenhower talking to Earl Warren in 1952 (this was when Warren was governor of California). Eisenhower is on the left.

In 1953 Eisenhower chose Earl Warren as Chief Justice of the Supreme Court. This was partly because he owed him a favour. Warren had stood aside during Eisenhower's campaign for the presidency and added crucial support to his successful election. Eisenhower later called this appointment 'the biggest mistake' of his presidency.

This small personal decision went on to have huge consequences for civil rights. The Supreme Court had previously been content to let the *Brown* case drift (see page 6). But Warren completely altered this situation by making sure that the *Brown* decision declared without a shadow of a doubt that educational segregation was morally wrong and unconstitutional. This created unwelcome problems for Eisenhower.

The *Brown* decision meant the federal government had to get involved in desegregation in the South – even though Eisenhower supported '**states' rights**'. This was a major wobble on Eisenhower's political tightrope walk!

States' rights: every state in the USA has its own laws. Generally speaking, the federal government only has the powers that have specifically been given to it by the US Constitution: everything else is governed by the state. Some Southerners claimed that they had states' rights to oppose federal law on desegregation.

Source B: Eisenhower comments privately on the *Brown* decision in May 1954.

> I am convinced that the Supreme Court decision set back progress in the South at least fifteen years…It's all very well to talk about school integration – if you remember that you may also be talking about social disintegration. Feelings are deep on this…We can't demand perfection in these moral things. All we can do is keep working towards a goal and keep it high. And the fellow who tries to tell me that you can do these things by FORCE is just plain NUTS

Eisenhower's frosty reception to the Supreme Court ruling encouraged Southern politicians to defy it. In 1955 the court issued the ruling again because it was being ignored. The president intervened to tone down the language and to prevent states having to follow the ruling by any set time. Various states took this to mean that the president was secretly in sympathy with their non-cooperation, or might at least turn a blind eye.

Activity

3. To what extent did President Eisenhower help *Brown v. Topeka* become such a major success for the civil rights movement?
   Think about:
   • Eisenhower's own views
   • his actions: intended and unintended.

Little Rock: protest and the president

Eisenhower was strongly against the federal government using force against state governments. But then came Little Rock (see page 8). Eisenhower was forced to send over 1,000 troops to the city to protect the nine black students from the angry white mob. If he hadn't:

- the US public would have held him responsible for what happened to the students
- federal law would have stood for nothing in the USA
- communist countries around the world would have had a major propaganda victory against the USA as 'defender of freedom'.

Eisenhower had been shamed into action by the protestors. Over the next three years he refused to pursue legal action against other states that also resisted educational integration. He also held back the FBI from investigating racial attacks in the South claiming he did not want to create a 'Gestapo around here'. Black activists were grateful for his almost accidental contribution to the *Brown* decision, but were rather scathing about his other actions.

Source C: Roy Wilkins, NAACP activist, gives his views on Eisenhower.

> President Eisenhower was a fine general and a good, decent man, but if he had fought World War II the way he fought for civil rights, we would all be speaking German today.

Activities

4. What evidence from these two pages and elsewhere would you use to argue that civil rights protests forced President Eisenhower to act in support of black civil rights?

5. What evidence from these two pages and elsewhere would you use to argue that Little Rock made Eisenhower determined to resist doing anything else to push black civil rights forward?

Kennedy: government and protest

John F. Kennedy is now remembered as a supporter of black civil rights. But it is important to remember that his party, the Democrats, had strong support from white people in the Southern states. Kennedy needed to appeal to segregationist Southerners as well as Northern liberals.

Kennedy was up against Richard Nixon for the presidential election in 1961. For the first time there were enough black people registered to vote to make a difference to election results. Both Kennedy and Nixon made promises to support civil rights, but Kennedy did a bit more. In 1960 he helped to free Martin Luther King from a four-month jail sentence after his arrest during a sit-in in Atlanta. In the presidential election, Kennedy only just won the vote: by 1%. But he got 70% of all the votes cast by black Americans.

Early presidency

Kennedy had come to power by promising big changes in civil rights. But it was never really possible to keep those promises:

- he had only a tiny majority in Congress so he had to try to keep everyone happy
- he needed the Southern Democrats in particular if he wanted the support of Congress
- if he did try to get Congress to support civil rights changes and they rejected it, there might be a risk of riots by black Americans.

It seemed safer for the moment to do nothing.

The Battle of 'Old Mississippi'

In 1961 a black US airforce veteran, James Meredith, had applied to the University of Mississippi (which was known as 'Ole Miss' – as in 'Old Mississippi'). Not realising that he was black, the university had accepted him. When they discovered Meredith was a black man, they made up any excuse they could think of to back out on the deal.

The NAACP took the case to court and in June 1962 a federal court ordered that Meredith be accepted at the university. The governor of Mississippi, Ross Barnett, made a speech designed to boost his own support among segregationist whites (see Source D).

Source D: Televised speech by Ross Barnett in 1962.

> No school will be integrated in Mississippi…There is no case in history where the Caucasian [white] race has survived social integration. We must…stand up like men and tell them, 'NEVER!'

Kennedy and his brother Robert tried to negotiate behind the scenes in the hope of avoiding bloodshed. Yet, on Meredith's first day on campus, about 3,000 racists attacked the university. This was despite a televised speech by Kennedy on the same day, stressing his support for the Court's decision. US marshals sent to protect Meredith were injured, two civilians were killed, and more than 300 people were arrested. Order was restored only after the president sent in 31,000 troops at a cost of $2.7 million.

Meredith was allowed to go to the college. But federal troops were stationed nearby in case of any trouble, and many students made Meredith's life in college as unpleasant as they could. Despite this, he graduated in 1963. Meredith's goal was to put pressure on JFK. Do you think he succeeded?

Activities

6. Compare Little Rock under Eisenhower and 'Ole Miss' under Kennedy. How did the two presidents respond to protest and opposition?

7. Work out arguments to support each of the statements below.

   - Kennedy only pretended that he was going to help the civil rights movement so black voters would help him get elected.
   - Kennedy wanted to help the civil rights movement but it was politically impossible to do it.
   - Kennedy could only push for civil rights changes when opponents to change went too far in their use of violence.

Birmingham protests

So Kennedy had actually done very little for civil rights before his final months as president. He had made some weak proposals to improve voting rights, but even these timid efforts were rejected by Congress. It was only as a direct result of the civil rights protests in Birmingham, Alabama, that Kennedy made a decisive move.

Martin Luther King's campaign in Birmingham (see page 16) gave Kennedy problems that could not be solved by compromise. The protestors set out to provoke national outrage in order to bring about real political change. Faced with the skilful negotiations of King and increasing public outrage at televised violence towards child protestors, Kennedy had little choice but to make a firm declaration.

Source E: Kennedy's televised speech to the nation following the Birmingham riots in 1963.

> We are confronted primarily with a moral issue…The heart of the question is whether all Americans are to be afforded [given] equal rights and equal opportunities; whether we are going to treat our fellow Americans as we want to be treated. If an American, because his skin is dark, cannot eat lunch in a restaurant open to the public; if he cannot send his children to the best public schools available; if he cannot vote for the public officials who represent him; if, in short, he cannot enjoy the full and free life which all of us want, then who among us would be content to have the color of his skin changed and stand in his place?…One hundred years of delay have passed since President Lincoln freed the slaves, yet their heirs, their grandsons, are not fully free. They are not yet freed from the bonds of injustice; they are not yet freed from social and economic oppression. And this nation…will not be fully free until all its citizens are free.

This speech made a firm commitment to civil rights legislation. The success of the March on Washington (see page 16) underlined the need for a change in the law. It was not clear, however, what precise shape these new laws would take. There was always the possibility, too, that Kennedy would back down on his promises as the pressure on him grew weaker. As it was, Kennedy's assassination in November 1963 meant we will never know for sure.

Source F: President Kennedy meets the leaders of the March on Washington in August 1963. Martin Luther King is second from the left and JFK is fourth from the right.

Activities

8. Study Source E. Explain why this speech was seen as a firm commitment by Kennedy to real action to help black civil rights.

9. Kennedy tried to negotiate with civil rights activists and opponents of reform 'behind the scenes'. He wanted to prevent violence and the media attention that came with it.
   - Was this a successful tactic for dealing with civil rights protest methods?
   - Why wasn't it possible to tackle the Birmingham situation this way?

10. Which of the following statements do you agree with and why?
   - President Kennedy and Martin Luther King are both famous for what they did for civil rights.
   - King is famous for his achievements; Kennedy for what he might have achieved for civil rights.
   - It is wrong to see Kennedy as someone who helped the civil rights movement.

ResultsPlus
Top Tip

For good marks in your controlled assessment, always include precise information to support your points.

Johnson: government and protest

President Johnson masterminded the Civil Rights Act of 1964 – the greatest advancement in black rights since the end of slavery in 1863. He pushed through this long-awaited legislation on the back of national mourning at the assassination of President Kennedy.

Source G: An extract from a televised speech by Johnson, five days after Kennedy's assassination.

> No memorial oration or eulogy could more eloquently honor President Kennedy's memory than the earliest possible passage of the Civil Rights Bill for which he fought so long.

The following year Johnson went further than perhaps Kennedy would have been willing to go. In response to the continuing problems faced by black people in registering to vote, Johnson sponsored the Voting Rights Act of 1965 (see page 18). These two laws were Johnson's greatest achievement but they also formed part of a wider vision that he believed necessary to bring about true social change.

The 'Great Society'

Johnson declared a 'war on poverty' and succeeded in pushing through new laws that he hoped would bring about a 'Great Society'. This included:

- cutting unemployment
- providing healthcare for the poor and needy
- clearing inner-city slums
- stimulating economic growth through reducing some taxes.

These programmes relied on large-scale government funding, a prosperous economy and the goodwill of the public.

But by the late 1960s the economy was not doing well and Johnson could no longer afford to support these ambitious social policies. Also, anti-Vietnam War protests, women's lib protests, the increasing social unrest in the inner-city areas and the rise of black nationalism and militancy (see pages 20–23) turned white public opinion away from 'Great Society' projects.

Activity

11. Which of these statements would you agree with and why? You can agree with more than one (or none).

- President Johnson was more important than civil rights protestors in getting the Civil Rights Act made law.
- President Johnson was only able to get the Civil Rights Act passed because of President Kennedy's work.
- The civil rights movement's effective non-violent protest made it inevitable that the Civil Rights Act would be passed one day.

Johnson: what went wrong?

Despite being the president who did the most for black civil rights since the ending of slavery, President Johnson faced a growing storm of protest about America's social problems. It must have been a great disappointment to Johnson that, despite having such high goals for American society, his efforts seemed only to open the floodgates to more unrest and conflict.

There were several factors that fractured Johnson's plans for a 'Great Society':

- the Vietnam War
- protests for equal rights for women
- a growing gap between the younger generation (especially students) and older people
- tensions with and within the civil rights movement
- social and economic changes in the USA
- inequality in US cities.

You can find out more about the problems Johnson faced, on pages 38–42.

Government and protest – a relationship?

Protest has got to make some positive connection with government if it is going to be effective. It is a bit like gears: they have to mesh in order to move things forward.

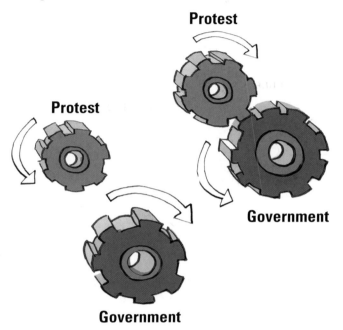

Protest

Protest

Government

Government

Although the civil rights protests were aimed at shaming presidents into action, and though presidents often did all they could to wriggle out of commitments and water down promises, something came out of the relationship that both sides could be proud of.

Also, the successes of the civil rights protests showed the way for other types of protest. Women's liberation protests, for example, made very good use of the media and campaigners achieved successes for women's rights in the Civil Rights Act of 1964 too. To an extent, the campaigns connected with the government's own ambitions and progress was made.

The situation with Vietnam did not work in the same way, however. The gears of Johnson's government and the anti-war protestors did not 'mesh'. President Johnson was convinced that America had to defend South Vietnam from communist North Vietnam, despite the protestors. In the end, the stress of this conflict contributed to Johnson's decision to stop being president.

Civil rights – a breakdown in the relationship?

In some ways, the relationship between the civil rights movement and the federal government broke down after 1965. One good example is that, after Martin Luther King began criticising the Vietnam War, Johnson refused to work with him.

This happened during the Chicago Freedom Movement of 1966, which was King's first attempt to bring non-violent protest methods to a Northern city to try to improve housing in black communities. This protest was a failure as:

- marches ended in violence
- white people in the North proved just as racist and violent as in the South
- white unions refused to help the protestors
- black people lost confidence in the protest and turned to more radical methods
- solving the housing problem required massive amounts of money which federal government didn't have because of the cost of the Vietnam War. By 1968 it had risen to $66 million a day.

The connection between the 'gears' of the presidency and the protestors started to slip and then to disengage. The protest methods of the 1950s and early 1960s failed to make headway against the massive problems of Northern cities. Perhaps Johnson thought that King was no longer such an effective force in the civil rights movement, and that is another reason why he cut the relationship.

Activity

12. Which of these factors do you think was the most important influence on the way the three presidents reacted to protests over civil rights – and why?
    - Media coverage of violence against black protestors.
    - Personal character: what the presidents' personalities were like.
    - Whether they would pick up lots of votes if they supported black issues.
    - Having people in the civil rights movement they could deal with.
    - How big a majority they had from the electorate (Johnson's was the biggest in US history in 1964).
    - The strength of the economy.

Government or protest – which was the driving force?

To pull this topic together, this final task looks at a key question for this chapter: who was driving change? Was it:

- the president and federal government, or
- the protestors?

It is a bit like the diagram of the gears on page 33 – which of the gears is the one that is driving the other?

For example, we have seen that the presidents were all very concerned about media coverage. When protests attracted lots of media coverage, especially if it involved violence against peaceful protestors, presidents usually had to act. Since we know that protest groups sometimes deliberately looked for ways to clash with the opposition, it looks as if the presidents were simply responding to the protests.

But then again, there were many protests that didn't result in big successes for the protestors. For example, *Brown v. Topeka* was not the first legal challenge to segregated schools – there was a long line of cases going back to 1849! The civil rights movement was a long, hard road. The same is true for the hundreds of massive demonstrations against the Vietnam War, the thousands of meetings, sit-ins, protest songs, letters and petitions (and votes) that demanded that the USA pull out of the war. Historians agree that, while presidents could not ignore this, they did not change their policy because of it.

So does that mean presidents acted only when it suited their purposes? Certainly, President Kennedy really threw his weight behind civil rights legislation after the March on Washington showed how popular the issue was across America. And Kennedy also found his relationship with Martin Luther King was politically very useful.

But that can't be the whole story either. We've seen how a successful protest often sparked off a whole series of other protests, or how a concession by the government then led immediately to further protests, such as when the Civil Rights Act was followed by protests about voting rights.

ResultsPlus
Top Tip

High marks are awarded to students who can show how factors work together to bring about progress.

Your conclusion so far

From this topic, we have seen:

- The three presidents all had different reactions to the protests of the civil rights movement.
- Eisenhower was reluctant to support civil rights but ended up overseeing major progress.
- Kennedy promised great changes but had very little room to manoeuvre.
- Johnson pushed through landmark laws only to see the protest movements threaten his vision for American society.

From what you have learned in this topic, explain whether you think progress in civil rights was driven more by presidents or movements.

When completing this task, think about which of the three presidents had the most influence on what happened, when it happened, and how it happened. You could:

- organise this question into a class debate
- write an answer to this question as a practice essay
- put together a Venn diagram with one circle representing one part of the question, one circle the other part of the question and, where they overlap, the cases where neither government nor protest seemed to be the driving force.

A4 Protest and dissent – mass protest and assassination as factors for change 1955–70

Learning outcomes

By the end of this topic, you should be able to:

- explain how three key assassinations affected the protests of the 1960s
- analyse the effects of mass protest and assassination
- evaluate the extent of change brought about as the result of mass protest and assassination.

Three significant deaths

JFK	Malcolm X	Martin Luther King

Effects of assassination

- Greater public awareness of the issues?

- Movement weakened without inspirational leader?

- Movement strengthened because followers more determined?

- Increased public support for aims because leader seen as martyr?

- Decreased public support because people are afraid?

- Change halted in response to such opposition?

The assassination of JFK

President Kennedy was shot in 1963 while visiting Dallas as part of his campaign for re-election. His assassination shocked the nation but it also focused attention on his policies.

Although Kennedy had shown support for the civil rights movement and for Martin Luther King personally, it was only after the Birmingham campaign that he committed himself to taking action (see page 31). President Johnson then used the shock of Kennedy's assassination to get new laws passed.

Assassination: murder of a public figure, often used to affect the political situation.

Activities

1. Why might people have felt it was difficult to criticise Kennedy's support for civil rights after his death?

2. Do you think Johnson would have felt he had to follow up Kennedy's policies before he tried to get his own ideas accepted?

Source A: The family of John F. Kennedy at his funeral.

The assassination of Malcolm X

Malcolm X's assassination by members of the Nation of Islam, while addressing a rally in New York in 1965, showed the lack of unity among the civil rights groups. Black Muslim mosques were set on fire in Harlem (a black area of New York) and in San Francisco by some of his followers.

In some press reports of the assassination he was presented as a martyr, with descriptions of the firebomb attack on his house a week earlier and of his comments in the previous months that he expected to be killed. Other reports focused on his background of crime and his radical preaching, for example the *New York Times* called him 'an extraordinary and twisted man', who had utilized his 'true gifts to evil purpose'. *Time* magazine said his 'gospel was hatred'.

However, his influence remained strong after his death, especially in the formation of the Black Panther Party in 1966. Huey Newton and Bobby Seale, who founded the BPP, wanted to continue Malcolm X's work for the black working class and his emphasis on self-defence and actual improvements in living conditions, rather than just changes in legal rights. He remains a key figure for many African-Americans, as was shown by Spike Lee's film, *Malcolm X*, released in 1992.

The assassination of Martin Luther King

Martin Luther King was assassinated in Memphis in April 1968. This had a major effect on the attitude of many black Americans and led to a violent backlash including riots across America (see page 20). Although Ralph Abernathy showed that the civil rights movement would continue by going ahead with the protests that King had organised such as the Poor People's Campaign (a march from Memphis to Washington), there was increasing support for the more aggressive attitude of Black Power.

By 1970, mass protests on the issue of civil rights were declining. This was because:

- King had been an excellent fundraiser and figurehead; without him to hold them together, the various organisations drifted apart
- the changing nature of the civil rights movement, especially the growth of Black Power, created an image of violence and gave the impression that white support was not welcomed
- concern was growing about the war in Vietnam so civil rights marches and protests were overshadowed.

Activities

3. In groups of four, discuss the effect of Malcolm X's assassination. One person should represent the views of each of the following groups:
   a) black followers of Martin Luther King
   b) members of the Black Panthers
   c) white civil rights supporters
   d) white people who want discrimination to continue.

4. Copy and complete the following chart.

	JFK	Malcolm X	MLK
Role in the civil rights movement			
Short-term effect of assassination			
Long-term effect of assassination			

5. Use the diagram on page 35 to explain whose death you think had most impact on the situation of black Americans in the 1960s.

Follow up your enquiry

Find a book or website about the civil rights movement and see how the deaths of these three are portrayed – does the account suggest that the civil rights movement sped up/slowed down or changed direction after their deaths?

Did assassination change anything?

The impact of assassination partly depends on the role played by the individual. As you have seen, Kennedy had done relatively little to help civil rights campaigners but in 1963 it seemed that he was about to become more active. Would he have achieved more than Johnson did, if he hadn't been assassinated, or was Johnson able to achieve so much *because* Kennedy had been assassinated?

When considering the effect of the assassinations of Malcolm X and Martin Luther King, you have to think about whether each of them was *a* leader or was *the* leader. For example, groups involved in the civil rights movement included CORE, NAACP, SNCC, SCLC and so on. It usually needs a single person to act as leader or it needs an event to bring different groups together, before their protests have much impact. So did Martin Luther King simply get the publicity and therefore overshadow others or was he genuinely important because his personal qualities could unite different groups? Would a different leader have used the same methods and got the same results?

Source B: From *Pursuing Life and Liberty, Equality in the USA 1945–68* by Bunce and Gallagher, a school textbook published in 2009.

> King's death became a symbol of the end of the civil rights movement... President Johnson called for a national day of mourning...More than 50,000 mourners joined King's funeral procession. Black Americans reacted violently. Racial violence broke out in 130 cities across 29 states…
>
> Malcolm X's significance was his ability to express the feelings of America's black working class. Following Malcolm X's assassination, the Organization of Afro-American Unity collapsed but many of its aims became central to other radical groups, particularly the Black Panther Party.

Mass protest

Mass protests are intended to show that large numbers of people want change, which puts pressure on the government to take action. Examples of mass protests are:

- 85% of Montgomery's black people boycotted the buses in 1955–56
- 70,000 people took part in sit-ins in the early 1960s
- at least 250,000 people marched on Washington in 1963.

The larger the scale of a protest, the more attention it is likely to gain from the media. This publicity then means that even more people are aware of the issues and expect the government to take action. If the protest gains negative international attention, the pressure on the government is intensified.

Mass protests usually aim to be peaceful because protestors do not want to give the government any excuse not to listen to their demands.

Source C: The March on Washington in 1963.

> **Mass protest:** A protest that involves lots of people, e.g. marches, petitions, boycotts.

ResultsPlus
Top Tip

When you research, make sure you make notes on specific details and keep a record of the author, book and page number, or website address. In your Part A Enquiry, the highest marks are reserved for answers which show evidence of personal research and make use of precise details, not generalised comments.

The 1960s featured many mass protests on a variety of issues. The largest mass protest happened in Washington DC in 1969, where almost 700,000 people gathered to protest against the Vietnam War.

Did you know?

Music was an important aspect of mass protests because songs can unite people and express their hope and determination. For example, marchers on civil rights protests often sang religious Negro spirituals, such as 'We Shall Overcome'.

What triggered the mass protests?

Throughout the 1950s the civil rights movement gained momentum. By the mid 1960s, the mass protests of the civil rights movement had:

- highlighted inequality and discrimination in American society. This led other people to examine their own lives and find injustice and inequality there
- showed that protests could be successful in bringing about change. It encouraged people to believe that they did not have to just accept the way things were
- attracted supporters from other liberal members of American society – especially students. These people learned how to protest successfully.

The mass protests of the 1960s can also be seen as a part of the 'counter-culture' of the time – a rebellion with a focus on the music, literature, fashion and art of youth. Many young people were rejecting some of the ideas and attitudes of their parents. The hippy movement was the most extreme form of this – hippies totally rejected established values and beliefs of society. However, the link to drugs and the idea of 'free love' meant that this aspect of youth culture was often called 'flower power' and not taken seriously.

Follow up your enquiry

Research the music festival held at Woodstock in 1969, which was billed as 'Three Days of Peace and Music' and attended by approximately half a million people.

Women's lib

The women's liberation movement felt that women were treated as second class citizens because the role of women in society seemed totally focused on the home and family. One of the most famous 'feminists' of the time was Betty Friedan, who published a book called *The Feminine Mystique* in 1963. She and other members of the women's liberation movement wanted:

- women to create an independent identity for themselves – through education and work, rather than through their husbands and family

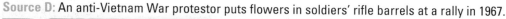

Source D: An anti-Vietnam War protestor puts flowers in soldiers' rifle barrels at a rally in 1967.

- more women to become active in public life
- better job and career opportunities, including for married women, most of whom still gave up work once they were married
- equal pay for working women
- to challenge stereotypical views of women and the emphasis on women's appearance which was reinforced by magazines, radio, TV programmes, advertising and film.

Feminists believed that women were trapped in this cycle.

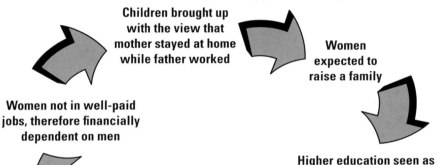

Children brought up with the view that mother stayed at home while father worked

Women expected to raise a family

Women not in well-paid jobs, therefore financially dependent on men

Lack of higher education meant women failed to get senior jobs

Higher education seen as a waste because women would stop working when they have a family

Activities

6. Study Source F and explain what point the protestors are trying to make.

7. What evidence is there that women based their protest methods on the ones used by the civil rights movement?

Source E: Marilyn Salzman Webb was a women's lib activist during the 1960s. Here she describes the attitude of her family towards her desire to attend medical school and become a doctor.

> I decided I wanted to be a doctor. My mother was against it. I remember her saying 'I should tell you this right from the start, girls are not doctors. We're not paying for you to go to medical school. If you went, you couldn't have a family.'…My grandfather…told my parents, 'Don't let her go away to college because then she won't be marriage material. She'll get ideas of her own.'

NOW

Friedan joined other feminists to set up the National Organization for Women (NOW) in 1966, reflecting the changed attitudes of the 1960s and the greater willingness to protest. NOW would use the experience many women had gained in the civil rights movement and anti-Vietnam War protests to try to influence public attitudes and government action through mass protests. The protests included marches, petitions, rallies, press conferences and media coverage. Slogans on posters included comments such as:

- Don't cook dinner: starve a rat today!
- End human sacrifice: don't get married!

Source F: A protest outside the 1968 Miss America beauty pageant in Atlantic City, New Jersey. As part of the protest, they binned their bras and crowned a sheep 'Miss America'.

What impact did the women's lib protests have?

The women's lib movement did achieve some successes.

- After Kennedy was elected president in 1961 he set up the Commission on the Status of Women. A result was the Equal Pay Act of June 1963.
- The 1964 Civil Rights Act made sexual, as well as racial, discrimination illegal.
- In 1967, President Johnson promised to appoint 50 women to top government posts and asked NOW for its advice.

It also generated a lot of publicity, so more people became aware of discrimination against women and acted against it.

Source G: This photograph of a protest in Washington in 1969, during Nixon's inauguration as president, shows how some women felt that they were still expected to fit their lives around their husbands.

However, there were limitations:

- In practice, it was difficult to enforce legislation and employers often ignored it.
- Much of the publicity generated was negative and women's lib activists were frequently presented as crazy, ugly and angry women who were protesting only because they could not find a man who would marry them!
- There was little improvement in the number of women employed in top professions or in politics (in 1969 there were still only 11 women senators in congress).

There were also major differences in the opinions of feminists themselves, which divided the movement.

Activities

8. Carry out some research so that you can copy and complete the chart below showing changes in women's role in society by 1970.

	Examples of changes made	Examples where changes were not made
Education		
Employment		
Social attitudes and expectations		
Legal rights		

9. Write a speech by a women's lib member to explain the situation in 1970 – decide whether this should be a positive or a negative view.

10. Explain whether the role of government was more important than the work of NOW in improving the situation for women.

11. The women's lib movement got a lot of publicity and some changes were made in law, so why did women still find it difficult to get equal pay and to progress to the top of their career at the end of the 1960s?

12. During the 1960s there were mass protests taking place by both the civil rights and women's lib movements. Do you think this would have increased or decreased their impact?

Yet more protests: the student sit-ins

In 1960 students at the University of Michigan formed Students for a Democratic Society (SDS). They were concerned about the inequalities in society between rich and poor and they developed links to the civil rights movement. The movement was fairly limited at first – the SDS had a total membership of 610 in October 1963. However, many students also wanted more say over the content of courses at college. In particular, a dispute arose in 1964 in Berkeley at the University of California where the college authorities tried to restrict student political activities, leading the students to form the Free Speech Movement.

Source H: From *Democracy's Children* by Edward K. Spann (2003).

> The affair reached a climax in December [1964], beginning with a call from FSM for another sit-in. Some 6,000 young people gathered for a mass rally in support of the protest. After listening to [the singer] Joan Baez…they heard [Mario] Savio urge them to bring the university to a stop…Then 800 protesters occupied Sproul Hall. The university responded by calling in the police, who cleared the hall, sometimes with brutal force…And there were mass arrests…The authorities won this battle but lost the war, for the student response was to initiate a strike that brought the university machine to a stop. Confronted with an organised rebellion within and much criticism from outside, the administration restored the customary right to free student speech in early 1965.

By 1966, there were 15,000 members of SDS and a number of smaller student organisations with similar aims of social equality and political freedom.

Hell no, we won't go!

There were many people who felt America should not be involved in the Vietnam War – either for moral reasons (because they thought the USA should not interfere in another country) or on practical grounds (because it was very expensive for the USA to make this commitment). When President Johnson committed troops to Vietnam and US soldiers became more directly involved in the fighting, the protests increased.

Many of the protests were organised and run by students although other sections of the public were also very active in the protests.

The war went badly for the USA; there were many casualties and the American public was shocked by media coverage of the war. Protests against the war included:

- people burning their **draft** cards and refusing to serve in the army
- marches, petitions and chants such as 'Hell no, we won't go!' and 'Hey, hey, LBJ, how many kids did you kill today?' (LBJ was Lyndon Baines Johnson – the president)
- sit-ins in public buildings where students were often supported by their lecturers giving 'teach-ins' about the Vietnam War.

The draft: the system by which young men between the ages of 18 and 25 were selected to serve in the US army.

Source I: The student Free Speech protest at Berkeley in 1964.

Activities

13. Why might it be easier to organise a mass protest on a university campus than in a town or city?

14. How much impact on the government and society do you think a student sit-in would have?

15. Some of the students involved in protests at Berkeley in 1964 had also been involved in Freedom Rides during the summer. How far do you think the student protests overlapped with the civil rights movement and women's lib?

Source J: A photograph of an anti-war protest in 1967; the man in the wheelchair is holding a poster saying 'My son died in vain. Don't fight! Go to prison'.

These protests did put pressure on both the universities and the government which was reinforced by the huge public reaction when a protest at Kent State University in 1970 led to the National Guard being called in and four students were shot dead.

Nevertheless, the actual impact of the anti-war protests is difficult to judge. Many historians feel that the protests were a factor in Johnson's decision not to stand for re-election in 1968. By the end of 1969, 34,000 'draft dodgers' were officially 'wanted' by the police. Yet, many Americans did not oppose the war – in fact, an opinion poll in 1970 produced a 50% response in favour of the war. Moreover, when a crowd of anti-war protestors was attacked by nearby construction workers in May 1970, people around them cheered.

Activities

16. Study Sources H and J. Compare the tactics used by these protestors with those used in the civil rights movement? How similar are they?

17. How far do you agree that student protests had less impact than civil rights protests?

Follow up your enquiry

Research the events at Kent State University in 1970 or investigate student protests at Berkeley.

Go to www.pearsonhotlinks.com, insert the express code 6459P and then click on 'student protests' to find some websites to get you started.

How much impact did mass protests actually have?

The source and activities that follow will help you evaluate the impact of mass protest.

Source K: From *America in White, Black and Gray*, by Klaus Fischer (2006).

> The most successful protest movement was the civil rights movement because its cause was widely recognized by most Americans as just and also because its tactics of peaceful resistance and moral sincerity made a deep impression on American public opinion.

Activities

18. Copy and complete the chart below, summarising the key changes during the period 1955–70. Explain which protest movement you think achieved the most.

	Civil rights	Women's lib	Student protest	Anti-Vietnam War protests
Changes 1955–60				
Changes 1961–65				
Changes 1966–70				

19. Why is it difficult to identify and evaluate the impact of mass protests?

20. Explain whether you think it was more important for protests to try to influence public opinion or to influence the government and which tactics were most effective in doing this.

Women's lib protests

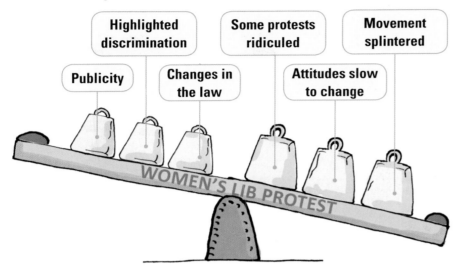

- Highlighted discrimination
- Some protests ridiculed
- Movement splintered
- Publicity
- Changes in the law
- Attitudes slow to change

WOMEN'S LIB PROTEST

ResultsPlus
Watch out

Protest songs were a key feature of the anti-war protests. Famous 'protest singers' include Bob Dylan, Joan Baez and Pete Seeger, while P.F. Sloan's 'Eve of Destruction' includes the line aimed at young men: 'You're old enough to kill but not for voting'. Although these songs were popular you cannot use them as evidence that they reflect popular attitudes. Many people sang along to Dylan's 'Blowing in the Wind' without agreeing with his views on the Vietnam War.

Activities

21. Draw two more seesaw diagrams showing the different aspects of the impact of civil rights protests and of anti-war protests. Make sure the angle of the seesaw shows how effective you think the mass protests were.

22. Imagine it is December 1968. In a group of four, hold an 'editorial meeting' for a newspaper to decide what should go on the front page of your review of the year. Explain whether you would focus on protests about civil rights, women's lib or the war in Vietnam, or the assassination of Martin Luther King.

Your conclusion so far

From this topic, we have seen that:

- The assassination of a leader can have both positive and negative effects, gaining publicity and creating additional support, speeding up a programme of events, or affecting the unity of supporters.

- Large-scale and well-publicised protests gained national attention, which was important because:
  - the national authorities could enforce changes to the law
  - the national authorities were concerned about the country's image in the international media and so more worried by negative publicity
  - mass protests gave the people involved a feeling of support and that they were not being ignored.

Protests which had very specific goals, such as the Montgomery Bus Boycott or the campaign to increase the number of registered black voters, were more obviously successful than protests trying to change government policy by campaigning for an end to US involvement in the Vietnam War or those trying to change attitudes, for example about racial or sexual discrimination.

From what you have learned in this topic so far, how far do you agree with Source K that the civil rights movement was the most successful protest movement?

To answer this question you need to:

- explain what was achieved by the civil rights movement, student protests, anti-Vietnam War protests and women's lib in terms of changes in the law and changing attitudes

- compare their achievements and see which protest movement was closest to achieving its aims.

Enquiry and writing skills support

Learning outcomes

By the end of this section, you should be able to:

- follow up an enquiry
- select and organise your material
- write up your enquiry.

In this section we will see how to complete the stages of following up an enquiry. The diagram on this page shows you the enquiry stages and what you need to do.

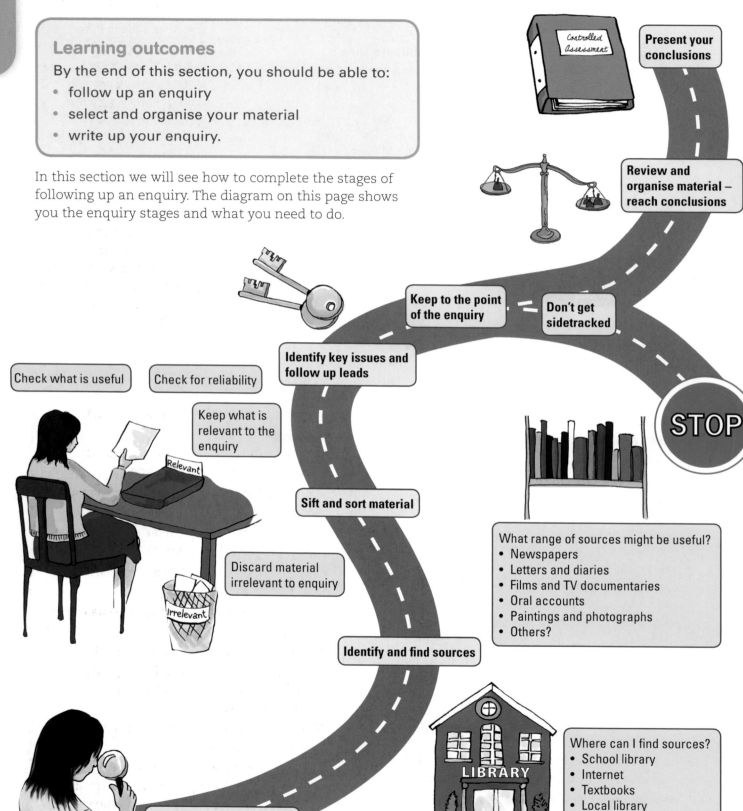

Present your conclusions

Review and organise material – reach conclusions

Keep to the point of the enquiry

Don't get sidetracked

Identify key issues and follow up leads

Check what is useful

Check for reliability

Keep what is relevant to the enquiry

Sift and sort material

Discard material irrelevant to enquiry

What range of sources might be useful?
- Newspapers
- Letters and diaries
- Films and TV documentaries
- Oral accounts
- Paintings and photographs
- Others?

Identify and find sources

Where can I find sources?
- School library
- Internet
- Textbooks
- Local library
- Others?

What is the enquiry about?

Following up an enquiry 1: Why did Lyndon Baines Johnson face so many protests during his presidency?

Your controlled assessment Part A task will be similar to this one:

> **Enquiry focus**
>
> The reasons why Lyndon Baines Johnson faced so many protests during his presidency.

In this practice example, we are going to follow up this enquiry focus. You will be able to use the skills you develop to follow up your own Part A enquiry.

What is the enquiry about?

Your first step is to identify the precise enquiry. In this instance it is asking why so many protests happened during Johnson's presidency. So your research is not about the details of the civil rights campaign or the anti-Vietnam War protests. This enquiry is trying to find out:

- what the major issues were that caused protest during Johnson's presidency
- why protests against several issues took place during this period.

Identify and find sources

The next stage is to gather your information. Start with an easy outline book and read through the relevant material. Write some summary notes, making sure you include the book title, author and the pages where you have found the information. You should only start to look for more detailed information when you have used two or three textbooks which give you the basic information.

Begin by re-reading pages 32 and 37–42 of this book.

You might start by doing a quick search on the internet but remember that many internet sites are just opinions without any factual support. This means that you should try only to use websites with endings such as org, com, ac, gov.

You should also look at books by historians. When you find a book, check the contents page and the index to make sure it covers the topic you want to research. Look up 'Johnson', 'protests', 'civil rights', 'students', 'Vietnam' and 'women's lib'.

You could also use TV documentaries as a source of information but be careful to check them against other sources to be sure they have not been too dramatised or exaggerated.

Sift and sort material

Go through your new sources and make additional notes. It will help if you use a fresh page for each book or other source. Remember your enquiry is about why Johnson faced so many protests, so a description of the protests will not be enough. Furthermore, the book or the webpage you've found was not written to answer your question! You have to think about what you read and choose what information to take – see Activity 1.

Activities

Making notes

1. Make a bullet point list of useful information, for example:
   - What protests were already an issue in 1963 when Johnson became president?
   - How did the civil rights protests develop during Johnson's presidency?
   - How did the student movement develop during Johnson's presidency?
   - Why did the Vietnam War protests become a problem for Johnson?
   - Why did women's lib become an issue at this time?

2. Colour code your points to show the role of individual leaders in coordinating these protests and the role of the media in publicising them.

3. Now repeat this process for two other textbooks or simple overviews.

4. Review the material you have researched so far and identify the key areas that you should go into in more depth or any gaps where you need to research more.

Source A: From *Race Relations in the USA* by Vivienne Sanders (2006).

> Johnson signed the civil rights bill in July 1964... However...blacks felt the act had not gone far enough. Most still suffered from poverty and discrimination. The weeks following the passage of the act saw riots in the black ghettos of many East Coast cities. Furthermore, the [mainly] black Mississippi Freedom Democratic Party (MFDP) demanded seats at the Democratic Party convention in Atlantic City, New Jersey, [claiming] that they were more representative than the segregationists...Johnson was outraged. He knew [this would mean the South would vote for the Republican Party in future].

Follow up leads

Source A tells you that Johnson's attempts to improve civil rights for black Americans did not end the protests:

- there was resentment from black people who felt that Johnson was not doing enough to end discrimination
- there was still great poverty in black communities
- there was rioting in many cities
- black people wanted further change to the political system.

So Johnson had not satisfied the civil rights movement. He had not achieved as much as he wanted in improving living and working conditions but black Americans wanted more political changes as well. At first they had just demanded the vote but now they wanted to be among the leaders of the Democrat Party.

You would need to go through the same process of finding, sifting and sorting, and noting information in order to consider these issues fully.

ResultsPlus

Top Tip

Looking for information can be a slow process. You might read through a lot to get a small piece of new information. But your work is better if you concentrate on what's new and relevant, rather than adding something that repeats information you already have or is not relevant.

Keep to the point of the enquiry

Don't go off track! On a journey, detours and side roads can be great fun and you can follow them up just because they are interesting. Remember, though, to return to your enquiry path – and not to add in material which isn't relevant, for example about Kennedy's assassination or events in the Vietnam War. This wouldn't help you answer your enquiry about why Johnson faced so many protests and it would just mean more work for you when you sort through all the material you have collected.

Source B: From *Democracy's Children* by Edward K. Spann (2003).

> The time of good feelings, however, soon gave way to increasing hostility and bitterness...[T]he years 1967 and 1968 marked a critical turning point in the history of the [1940s] generation. Many abandoned their hopes for democracy and the belief that they could bring about changes in society and government, which they had held previously.
>
> What had gone wrong? Part of the answer probably lay in the rapid growth of the protest organizations caused by the [way America's involvement in the Vietnam War was escalating]. Antiwar protests seemed by 1967 to have had little effect in persuading those in authority to slow the bloody pace of the Vietnam War...
>
> By 1967 over half the black people in America were under twenty-one. The attitudes of this new generation had been shaped by the civil rights movement and the expectations it raised. [Young black Americans focused on] the distance yet to be travelled to freedom rather than the distance already covered, and they found much reason for discontent. The abolition of discrimination by law was a basic triumph for American democracy, but [in practice, it] did little to improve the conditions of the black poor...
>
> For SNCC leaders and other young blacks, this situation demanded a radically new set of tactics...

Activities

Selecting information

5. Read Source B and decide with a partner how much of it is useful. Remember:
   - you want to find out why civil rights protests continued under Johnson and why there were other protests at this time
   - you also want to find out whether there were any links between the civil rights protests and the other protests
   - usually you want only new points
   - sometimes you may want to make a note that two sources agree about an important point.

6. Copy the whole passage. Colour code it: green for new information about civil rights protests; yellow for other protests and blue for repeated information. Some parts have been done for you.

Use sources carefully

So far we have applied two tests when using sources – relevance and duplication. You will also need to think about reliability. You need to be particularly careful about internet sources because they are sometimes anonymous and it is difficult to check the information they contain. Often too they are campaigning, and you need to think about their purpose and possible bias. As you use your sources, apply the RDR tests: relevance, duplication and reliability.

The text in Source B is relevant to this enquiry because it shows:

- the group most likely to be affected by the draft
- the different expectations from older generations
- those more likely to be influenced by the Black Power movement.

ResultsPlus

Top Tip

You will get better marks for your Part A enquiry if you refer specifically to sources you have read. For example, instead of saying 'some historians', include the actual name of the author. You can also use a short quotation.

Source C: From an article in the *Los Angeles Times* in August 2005. These comments are from Tommy Jacquette about the 1965 Watts riots in Los Angeles; he was 21 at the time.

> People keep calling it a riot, but we call it a revolt because it had a legitimate purpose. It was a response to police brutality and social exploitation of a community and of a people…A riot is a drunken brawl at USC because they lost a football game.
>
> People said that we burned down our community. No, we didn't. We had a revolt in our community against those people who were in here trying to exploit and oppress us.
>
> We did not own this community. We did not own the businesses in this community. We did not own the majority of the housing in this community.
>
> Some people want to know if I think it was really worth it. I think any time people stand up for their rights, it's worth it.

Activities

Relevance and reliability

7. Study Source C. It is from an article in the *Los Angeles Times* in August 2005, looking back at the Watts riots of 1965.

   Decide with a partner which of these statements you agree with. Choose as many as you like:

   (a) It is sympathetic to police.

   (b) It is sympathetic to the rioters.

   (c) It uses emotive language and comments.

   (d) It is not biased.

   (e) It is biased but still has some useful information.

   (f) It probably reflects the author's views during the 1965 riots.

   (g) His views might have been affected by events since 1965.

   (h) It tells us how all black people felt at the time.

   (i) It is mainly relevant to my enquiry.

   (j) It does not add much to my enquiry.

8. Add any useful information to your notes.

Identify key issues

Activities

9. Study Source D. It gives you two new leads for your enquiry about Johnson's problems: student protests against the USA's involvement in the Vietnam War and the importance of changing attitudes.

10. Add information from Source D to your enquiry folder. When you do your own research, it will help if you add page numbers, in case you want to find the passage again.

11. Begin to organise your information under key headings whenever you use a new source. Your enquiry has already given you the following leads and you could use these as headings or you could create other headings of your own.
    - Reasons why civil rights campaigns continued
    - Reasons why students protested
    - Reasons why there were protests against the Vietnam War
    - Reasons why women's lib protests were made at this time
    - Role of the media in publicising protests.

Source D: From *Coming Apart* by William L. O'Neill (1971).

The teach-ins…began at the University of Michigan on March 24, 1965 [where a] faculty…decided to have an all-night meeting…More than three thousand students attended…

The idea was contagious. Before long, almost every large university, and many small ones, held teach-ins. Berkeley's was, of course, the most spectacular. It went on for two days. Twelve thousand students heard…countless [speakers] denounce the war…

The teach-ins did not change the government's policy [but they] made dissent more respectable. Before them, many people who disliked the war were afraid to say so.

Follow up more leads

You now have a number of leads. Follow them up, using the source file and other useful sources you have found. Look back at page 44 to keep yourself on track.

Source E: From *America Divided*, by Isserman and Kazin (2000).

In 1965 civil rights leaders felt the time for caution was over. King and other leaders had learned that creating a crisis would dramatise the issue for a national audience. They chose Selma as the target for their voter registration campaign. Non-violent persuasion had got nowhere but non-violent provocation had real potential for media coverage.

Sheriff Clark lost his cool – just as SCLC strategists had hoped he would. He repeatedly managed to get his face on the front page of northern newspapers and on evening television broadcasts, as he beat protesters into submission and punched black ministers in the face. As the violence escalated, a march from Selma to Montgomery was organised. ABC News interrupted the network's Sunday night movie to show 15 minutes of raw and dramatic footage from the attack on the marchers.

In the days that followed, a white minister from Boston who joined the march was set upon by four local whites and died the next day from his injuries. Protesters marched outside the White House, demanding federal action.

Source F: From *Democracy's Children*, by Edward K. Spann (2003).

Black Power challenged [the] expectations that blacks would simply be integrated into a largely white society…[It]was born in a time of conflict, a time not simply of the war in Vietnam but also of a series of ghetto riots that intensified the new aggressiveness of young blacks…

From 1964 to the end of 1968, at least 329 serious riots in 257 cities produced a total of 52,629 arrests, 8,371 injuries and 220 deaths. In Los Angeles, Chicago, Detroit and Newark especially, the riots threatened to become open wars between law enforcement agencies and…bands of [young] black men.

Source G: From the website of the American PBS broadcasting company, in an article about John Gardner, one of President Johnson's officials.

President Johnson wanted to create the 'Great Society' – to end poverty, promote equality, improve education, rejuvenate cities, and protect the environment. Yet, the Great Society and Johnson's 'War on Poverty' had their critics. Some said that it…wasted money on hand-outs to people who did not deserve them. At the same time, Johnson's insistence [on] American involvement in Vietnam while spending billions of dollars on domestic problems placed a large strain on the economy.

Source H: From *And The Crooked Places Made Straight*, by David Chalmers (1991).

[In 1968] the CBS anchorman, Walter Cronkite went to Vietnam to have a look for himself. On his return, he presented a half hour 'special' on the war…His message was that…'It seems now more certain than ever… that the bloody experience of Vietnam is to end in a stalemate.'…President Johnson reportedly [said] 'Well, if I've lost Cronkite, I've lost Middle America.'

Source I: From *America in White, Black and Gray* by Klaus Fischer (2006).

The black civil rights movement was like a rolling stone that set in motion other national protests: antiwar demonstrations, student protests, the feminist movement, hippie power…among others. It furnished the rhetorical slogans and the tactics of protest: sit-ins, marches, demonstrations…boycotts, etc.

Reaching conclusions

You will need to decide why Johnson faced so many protests. Was he just unlucky that several issues became important at once? Did the achievements of the civil rights movement encourage other movements to use mass protest? Did the role of the media encourage demonstrations? What other factors affected the situation?

You could summarise your key points in an ideas map like the one below. Add different-coloured arrows to link the protests where publicity and the media were important, and to show where economic problems or other groups in society affected the situation.

Review and organise material – reach conclusions

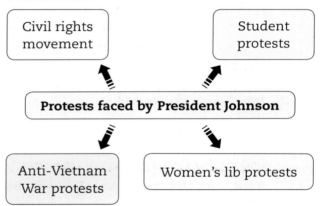

Present your conclusions

Activities

This activity is practice for your controlled assessment task.

12. Make a set of notes to go with your ideas map. Use the same headings. Do not use more than two sides of paper. You can include quotations from your sources in your notes. When you write up your work, make sure you explain why they are important in your answer.

13. Write up your enquiry: Why did Johnson face so many protests during his presidency? Afterwards, turn to Maximise your marks on pages 72–73 to see if your answer can be improved.

Following up an enquiry 2: Changes in the methods of protest – compare the Montgomery Bus Boycott of 1955–56 and the Black Panthers' 'Patrol the Pigs' campaign in 1967

This practice enquiry is different from enquiry 1. Enquiry 1 focused on causation and asked you to find out why Johnson faced so many protests during his presidency. This enquiry gives you practice in making comparisons and deciding how much methods of protest changed.

Follow the enquiry stages outlined on pages 44–45: identify your enquiry and your sources; sift and sort your information.

Begin by using pages 10–11 and 22 of this book. Then go on to the information given in the source file opposite. You can then follow up more leads if you like.

When you follow up your leads, don't forget to stick to the enquiry stages shown in the diagram on page 44, which you followed in enquiry 1. You can find accounts from eyewitnesses of events but you must use them with caution because many of them will have strong feelings about what they saw. This may affect the reliability of what they say. Also many people's opinions were influenced by their views about black people and discrimination and also about the use of violence. For example, Martin Luther King was prepared to use 'direct non-violent action' whereas Malcolm X suggested violence was acceptable. Can you tell from Source F that the author does not approve of the methods used by the Black Panther Party?

Activities

Making and sorting notes

14. Read pages 10–11 and 22 and the source file. Make a bullet point list of useful information, for example:

Montgomery Bus Boycott 1955–56

- Started when Rosa Parks refused to give up her seat on a bus.
- Whole black community refused to use the buses.
- Police attempted to intimidate the people involved.
- Violent attack also made on Dr King's home.
- Supreme Court ordered the state and bus company to change their rules.

15. Begin to organise your notes. For each protest, you could arrange them into a chart like the one below. Notes on the bus boycott have been started for you. Add details under each heading in the chart. You can also add new bullet points.

	Target of protest	Leaders	Actions	Effect of protest
Montgomery Bus Boycott	Discrimination in seating on buses to end	Leaders of local community planned the protest and chose MLK to lead it		Supreme Court declared segregated buses were illegal
'Patrol the Pigs' campaign				

16. Now colour code your chart. Use green for when protest methods were similar and red for different methods.

17. Finally, think about how much difference you can see between these two protests.

Source file

Source A: From a website celebrating the legacy of Martin Luther King.

It was an 'established rule' in the American south (at that time) that African-American riders had to sit at the back of the bus [and] to surrender their seat to a white bus rider if it was needed.

Mrs. Rosa Parks refused when she was asked to move to let a white bus rider be seated. She did not argue and she did not move. The police were called and Mrs. Parks was arrested.

Mrs. Parks was not the first African-American to be arrested for this 'crime'. But she was the first to be arrested who was well known in the Montgomery African-American community…

On the morning of Dec. 5, the African-American residents of the city refused to use the buses. Most walked, those few with cars arranged rides for friends and strangers, some even rode mules…As the boycott continued, the white community fought back with terrorism and harassment. The car-pool drivers were arrested for picking up hitchhikers. African-Americans waiting on street corners for a ride were arrested for loitering.

On January 30, 1956 Dr. King's home was bombed. His wife and their baby daughter escaped without injury…[and he said] *'We must learn to meet hate with love'.*

The boycott continued for over a year, until the Supreme Court declared that Alabama's state and local laws requiring segregation on buses were illegal. On December 20th federal injunctions were served on the city and bus company officials forcing them to follow the Supreme Court's ruling…The boycott had lasted 381 days. The boycott was a success.

Source B: From a 2007 article in *The Socialist Worker* about the Black Panthers.

From 1964 to 1968, black people rose up in almost every city in the north east, the Midwest and California. When the Watts ghetto in Los Angeles exploded in rage in 1965, the authorities deployed 15,000 armed police and National Guards. In the repression that followed 34 people died and 4,000 were arrested…

[Huey P Newton and Bobby Seale, leaders of the Black Panthers] found King's stress on non violence and his demand for integration into 'white society' too meek. [They preferred the ideas of] Malcolm X, [who] rejected the notion of integration in favour of 'black pride' – and [who] argued for the defence of black communities 'by any means necessary'…

[Newton] and Seale decided that one of the first objectives of the Panthers would be to end police harassment in their community. They recruited and armed young men and women to 'patrol the pigs' – following police patrols through the ghettos of Oakland…

Unsurprisingly, the state did not accept the right of the Panthers to patrol the police, let alone to do so with their own arms and uniform [and a new law was proposed in 1967] to outlaw the carrying of loaded weapons. The Panthers responded by organising an armed march on the state capital.

Bobby Seale recalled…'There were 30 brothers and sisters – 20 of the brothers were armed…' California's governor, Ronald Reagan, who was on the lawn… took one look and ran. In front of hundreds of reporters, Bobby Seale read a proclamation that put the Panthers on the national map.

Within months of the protest, the party grew from about 50 members to over 5,000, as new activists joined and started operations in towns and cities across the US.

Source C: From Bunce and Gallagher, *Pursuing Life and Liberty, Equality in the USA 1945–1968*, a school textbook published in 2009.

One of the Panthers' first initiatives was the 'patrol the pigs' campaign, which began in Oakland, California. Essentially the campaign was designed to keep the police under surveillance, in order to protect African Americans from the abuse of police power. Any time a police patrol [car] stopped…an African American, Black Panther patrols would observe the incident. Newton…carried law books in his car and would intervene in any incident, questioning the police and drawing a crowd of onlookers. The campaign highlighted police abuses and educated local black residents about their legal rights.

Source D: From *And the Crooked Places Made Straight*, by David Chalmers (1991).

> When their boycott began, the black people of Montgomery asked only to be treated politely, and they were refused…[They used] peaceful confrontation and a willingness to suffer violence and imprisonment [when they] publicly [broke] unjust laws. The basic inspiration came from Christianity [and] the black churches…King sought to change the attitude of the white majority by forcing it to face the moral issue of segregation and discrimination…National attention had been focused on race relations in the South…

Source F: From *America in White, Black and Gray* by Klaus Fischer (2006).

> Malcolm X's followers…[included] Stokely Carmichael…Eldridge Cleaver, Huey Newton, and Bobby Seale…these radical activists were united in their hatred of white America…No longer content to demonstrate peacefully, they advocated striking back at their oppressors. This turn towards black power developed in 1965 and 1966.
>
> The most feared black group…was the Black Panther Party…The party recruited primarily street thugs…and delighted in confronting the hated white establishment, especially its police 'pigs'.

Source E: From *Coming Apart*, by William L. O'Neil (1971).

> Being devoted to the Bible, Southern blacks grasped the idea of nonviolence readily. And as they were so heavily outnumbered and even more outgunned, nonviolence was the obvious response. It is what the weak use to turn the oppressor's strength against him. White Southerners were slow to understand this. At first they met nonviolent demonstrations with force. This produced martyrs, strengthened the movement, and won outside support…

Source G: From the History Learning website.

> The Black Panthers were formed in California in 1966 and they played a short but important part in the civil rights movement. The Black Panthers believed that the non-violent campaign of Martin Luther King had failed…The language of the Black Panthers was violent as was their public stance. The two founders… Huey Percy Newton and Bobby Seale, [p]reached for a 'revolutionary war'…They were willing to use violence to get what they wanted…
>
> To view the BPP as a purely revolutionary and violent movement is wrong. In areas of support the BPP created a Free Food Program to feed those who could not afford to do so for themselves; Free Medical Research Health Clinics to provide basic health care for those who could not afford it and a…Youth Band [gave] community pride to the movement…

Writing up your answer

The moderator will be looking for four main things – that you have:

- kept your answer focused on the enquiry
- found information from different sources
- backed up your statements with information
- communicated your answer by organising it well and using good spelling, punctuation and grammar.

The activities which follow will help you to improve your writing. Remember to use the skills you have learned when you write up your controlled assessment answer.

Activities

Improving writing

18. Imagine you are the moderator. Study example extracts 1 and 2 and discuss with a partner their good and bad points. (Answers are at the bottom of page 53.)

19. Suggest ways you could improve examples 1 and 2. You can do this in bullet point notes.

20. Study example 3. It is part of a high-level response. It compares methods, finding similarities and differences, and giving details. Now try adding to the answer by giving examples to support the statement at the end of the second paragraph. You can also add more paragraphs giving similarities and differences.

Example extract 1

They were very similar. Both protests wanted to get publicity for the poor treatment of black people. The Montgomery Bus Boycott was complaining about how unfairly black people were treated on the buses and the Black Panther group thought the police acted unfairly. In both protests they hoped that they could show how united the black people were and they thought that would change the situation.

Example extract 2

The Montgomery Bus Boycott was just about one particular issue. It started when Rosa Parks refused to give up her seat to a white person. This was a very unfair situation because the bus had 'black' seats and 'white' seats but if all the white seats were taken, the black people had to stand and the whites would take their seats.

The black community united in protest and stopped using the buses. They would share cars or walk and sometimes white women would drive their black maids rather than have to clean their house themselves. The boycott was an economic protest because it reduced the amount of profit the bus company could make.

The Black Panther 'patrol the pigs' protest was about a wider issue – unfair treatment from the police. Like the bus boycott, it aimed to get attention and unite the black community but it used different methods and was more aggressive.

Example extract 3

Although both protests had the same basic aim of getting a change made through highlighting the 'wrong' aspects of the way black people were treated, the leaders of the protests had very different attitudes towards the authorities and therefore their attitudes towards the use of violence were also different.

The bus boycott was non-violent and did not attack the authorities. This is shown very clearly in "And the Crooked Places Made Straight" where David Chalmers says that they aimed to use their suffering to draw attention to the unfair laws. In contrast, we know that the Black Panthers were prepared to confront the authorities and to use violence. [The answer gives further examples, quoting sources.]

Another aspect of the protests that was similar was the 'emphasis on a community working together to help each other. The idea behind the Black Panthers' 'Patrol the Pigs' was to have people from the black community who were able to ensure the police were not discriminating against them, while the account on the website http://www.watson.org/~lisa/blackhistory/civilrights-55-65/montbus.html tells me that the leaders of the bus boycott set up a committee to organise shared rides so that the black people could still get to work.

However, there were important differences. The bus boycott was planned. The organisers obviously wanted to carry this protest out but had to wait for the 'right' victim. It suggests that Rosa Parks was a good case to use because she was well respected in the black community and this helped to unite them. Bunce and Gallagher suggest the Black Panthers were much less organised and more spontaneous. They planned their approach and actually followed the police, looking for any excuse to get involved but at the same time, there was no overall plan on how to deal with individual cases, they just reacted to each one as it happened. The Black Panthers also did not make any single case an issue to unite the whole community, whereas the treatment of Rosa Parks was deliberately chosen as a symbolic case and intentionally publicised...

Example one does identify similarities, but it is not detailed enough and it does not identify any differences.

Example two has more detail and has made some comments about similarity and difference. But the student has got side-tracked. The answer is partly about the reason for the bus boycott rather than the methods.

Neither example 1 nor example 2 refers to any sources.

Summary

Success in your enquiry comes from:

- sticking to the focus of the enquiry
- using a range of sources, keeping their relevance and reliability in mind
- organising your answer to show good quality of written communication.

Part B Representations of history

What was the impact of mass protest on US society 1955–70?

In Part B of your controlled assessment you are exploring the impact of mass protests and assessing how much they achieved. The aim of this chapter is to understand why historians develop different opinions about the success of these tactics.

Who cared about mass protests?

The point of a mass protest is that, by showing how many people want change, pressure will be placed on the authorities to take action. Therefore publicity is a very important aspect of this tactic. In one way this is very helpful for the historian – we have lots of evidence to tell us what people were complaining about and also to tell us how the protests were carried out.

However, it is more difficult to find out what *effect* mass protests had. There is usually evidence to show the reaction of the authorities – for example President Kennedy said he was 'sickened' by photographs of the events in Birmingham in 1963 and announced his support for a new law aimed at ending segregation. However, we do not always know how ordinary people reacted.

In November 1969, President Nixon used the phrase 'silent majority' when talking about attitudes to the war in Vietnam. He suggested that although protestors got a lot of attention, they were only a small section of society and did not properly represent public attitudes. The poster held by protestors in Source A challenges that comment. The historian's problem is how can he or she be sure the evidence they select really does reflect public opinion?

Source A: An anti-Vietnam War protest march in 1969.

Activities

1. Publicity for new films often includes positive comments from film critics. Discuss how easy it would be to check whether people who saw the film agreed with those views.

2. What tactics can a protest group use to give the impression that many people agree with their views?

3. Explain the difficulties involved in finding out the views of 'the silent majority'.

4. Explain how media reports can make a protest seem important or trivial, depending on how it is presented.

Evidence of attitudes

The historian needs to be aware that evidence about the impact of the Montgomery Bus Boycott will be easier to find than evidence about the impact of the women's lib protest at the 1968 Miss America Pageant. In the case of the Montgomery Bus Boycott, the fact that the buses were desegregated suggests the protest was successful. However, it is far more difficult to assess what effect the women's lib protest had – it gained publicity but did it change attitudes or lead to an improvement in women's status in society?

The historian needs to think about whether campaigns with specific, short-term goals, such as the Montgomery Bus Boycott, Little Rock High School, voter registration and so on, are more likely to appear to have an effect than campaigns which try to change attitudes, such as women's lib or the anti-Vietnam War movements.

ResultsPlus

Watch out

Remember that people's actions do not always give us a clear indication of their attitudes. Some people might have agreed with the protestors but be afraid to join in because of fear of violence or victimisation. Other people might not join in because they don't feel strongly about the issue or because they are too occupied with other aspects of their lives.

To help you to understand whether mass protests had an effect on public attitudes, you would need to consult a range of sources but you would also need some way of assessing how representative the views were.

Source B: The results of a series of public opinion polls during the 1960s.

The USA's mood:
The public's view of the most important problem facing the country, according to Gallup Poll results 1961–68

1961	Prices and inflation
1962	War, peace and international problems
1963	Racial problems
1964	Integration
1965	Vietnam
1966	Vietnam
1967	Vietnam
1968	Vietnam

The table in Source B suggests that most people saw Vietnam as the key issue during the 1960s but Source C shows that there was great variety in people's attitudes towards the Vietnam War.

Source C: A graph showing changing views of Nixon's handling of the Vietnam War.

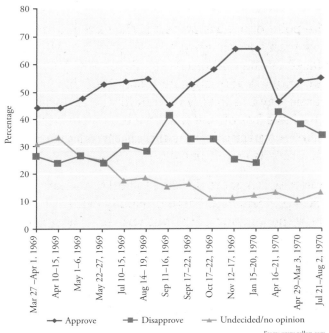

From: www.gallup.com

Activities

5. Explain the value and limitations of using each of the following sources to investigate public reaction to anti-Vietnam War protests in 1968.
   - A diary account from a protestor who was involved in the sit-in at Columbia University, New York, in April 1968.
   - An official report from a policeman at the Democratic Convention in Chicago in 1968 when the Students for a Democratic Society created a riot as a way of protesting about the pro-war views of Hubert Humphrey, a Democratic Party candidate.
   - A newspaper account of a draft-burning protest (see page 41).
   - A televised interview with the state governor, where he is asked about events during the year.
6. Explain how far you think it is possible for the historian to find out the views of the 'silent majority'.

Interpretations of mass protests

You have already seen that Martin Luther King used mass protests to campaign for improved civil rights but the historian also wants to assess the impact or effect of King's use of mass protests. While it is fairly easy to see the amount of publicity the protests received, it is far less straightforward to decide whether the protests actually brought about change. You know that the Montgomery Bus Boycott was successful in desegregating buses but Source D shows that unemployment among black males remained far higher than the average rate for all men, suggesting the mass protests were not very successful in improving employment opportunities.

Source D: A graph showing unemployment during the 1960s.

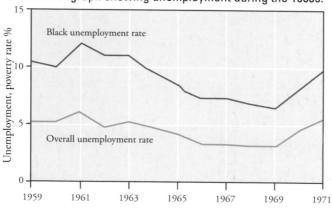

The following two sources show very different views of Martin Luther King and the impact of mass protests.

Source E: Taken from the Nobel Prize website, explaining why King was awarded a Nobel Peace Prize in 1964.

> [King] led a massive protest in Birmingham, Alabama, that caught the attention of the entire world…; he planned the drives in Alabama for the registration of Negroes as voters; he directed the peaceful march on Washington, D.C., of 250,000 people to whom he delivered his address, 'I Have a Dream', he conferred with President John F. Kennedy and campaigned for President Lyndon B. Johnson…and became not only the symbolic leader of American blacks but also a world figure.

Source F: From *Revolutionary Suicide* by Huey Newton, published in 1973. Here he is talking about the formation of the Black Panthers in 1966, after the riots in the Watts area of Los Angeles in 1965.

> We had seen Watts rise up the previous year. We had seen how the police attacked the Watts community after causing the trouble in the first place. We had seen Martin Luther King come to Watts in an effort to calm the people and we had seen his philosophy of nonviolence rejected…
>
> What good…was non-violence when the police were determined to rule by force? We had seen all this, and we recognized that the rising consciousness of Black people was almost at the point of explosion. Out of this need sprang the Black Panther Party.

Activity

7. Copy the diagram below and add in details for each aspect of improvements in the situation of black people that can be directly linked to a mass protest.

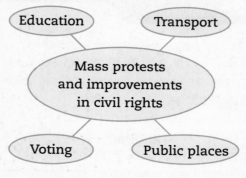

Activities

8. Study Source E. How does the author suggest that these mass protests played an important role in the civil rights movement?

9. Why do you think Source E does not mention that King's use of mass protests was criticised by both white and black people?

10. Use Source F to explain why some historians might say that Martin Luther King's use of mass protests was a failure.

11. In pairs, prepare a brief bullet point list about Martin Luther King's use of mass protests.

   Next, you should each write a paragraph about his use of mass protests. Although you should both use all of the points you have just identified, one of you should emphasise the positive points in order to present this as a successful tactic, while the other one should emphasise the negative points, suggesting it was a failure.

12. Explain what you think the historian should do when the evidence is contradictory:

   • choose which sources to believe and ignore the others
   • write an account which describes the views on both sides and avoid making a judgement
   • look for more sources and accept the majority view
   • weigh up the evidence and make a judgement.

Understanding attitudes

Racism

In our multicultural society we take it for granted that all people are equal. Yet historians must try to ignore their own views and understand the values and attitudes of the people at the time. For example, historians need to try to explain why the white students in Source G thought their behaviour was acceptable.

The historian also needs to understand that many people who did not view themselves as racist would still have used words like 'Nigger' and genuinely thought that black people were more suited to sport and music than to academic study. The historian does not need to agree with these views but he should be prepared to accept that they were common during the 1960s.

ResultsPlus
Top Tip

The decision to select or omit particular details and the way in which information is presented can create a particular impression. When historians are faced with conflicting sources, they need to check carefully whether they actually contradict each other or just have a different approach.

Source G: A professor and two students on a sit-in at a Woolworths lunch counter in Jackson, Mississippi. The dark stain on Professor Salter's shirt is blood. He was hit repeatedly with a piece of wood.

Source H: Taken from *Pursuing Life and Liberty: Equality in the USA 1945–68,* Bunce and Gallagher, 2009.

> In general terms the majority of Americans supported an end to legal segregation in the late 1960s. However, the majority of whites did not want to live in integrated neighbourhoods.

The historian needs to understand both the frustration and impatience that led many black people to feel that violence was acceptable, and also the views of the authorities who felt that mass protests threatened the whole of society and needed to be controlled. When Malcolm X and the Black Panthers raised ideas such as black separatism, many white people who had previously supported the civil rights movement felt that their support was now being rejected.

Source I: A New York taxi driver, talking about Malcolm X in 1961.

> [T]hose Black Muslims… make more sense than the NAACP and all the rest of them put together. They're for their own people and that Malcolm ain't afraid to tell the FBI or the cops where to get off. You don't see him pussyfootin' around the whites like he's scared of them.

Most historians are sympathetic to the black civil rights movement and will emphasise the unjust way black people were treated. However, historians have different views: on whether Martin Luther King's tactics were right, on the Nation of Islam's demand for a separatist state, on the Black Panthers' approval of violence. Their views on these issues will affect the way they write about the events and people involved.

Activity

13. Draw a longer version of the line below and place a mark on it to represent the views of each of the following people:

- the white students in Source G pouring things over the black students
- the white students in Source G watching what is happening
- the white people whose attitude is described in Source H
- the taxi driver in Source I.

Segregation and hatred ⟷ **Integration and tolerance**

Activity

14. Discussion: is it possible for a modern historian to write a fair explanation of racist views during the 1960s?

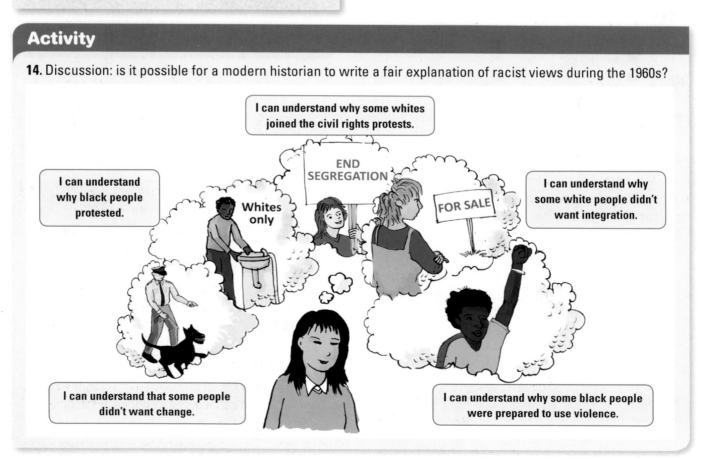

Feminism

The women's lib campaigners were often ridiculed and accused of being 'unfeminine'. The suggestion was sometimes made that they were only women's 'libbers' because they 'couldn't get a man'.

This is not a view that a modern historian would share but the historian needs to understand the way that many articles and advertisements in the 1960s continued to assume that a woman's only aim in life was to get married, run the home and have a family.

Source J: An advertisement for a washing machine during the 1960s.

Anti-Vietnam War protests

Anti-Vietnam War protests aroused similarly strong views. People opposing the war were accused of being disloyal to their country, or of being communists (who were seen as anti-American). This was especially felt to be true when protestors burned the American flag.

Source K: Senator John Stennis commenting about an anti-Vietnam War protest march in 1967.

It is clear…that this is a part of a move by the Communists…to divide the American people, disrupt our war effort, discredit our government before the entire world…Those who participate in these demonstrations tomorrow will be, in effect, cooperating with and assisting our enemy.

Source L: Alison Krause died from a shot fired during the protest at Kent State University in Ohio. Doris Krause, Alison's mother, is writing here about how people reacted to her daughter's death.

We got a condolence letter from President Nixon. Clearly it was written out of duty and not out of genuine sympathy. Just before the shootings he had referred to the students as 'bums'. The day after she was killed, my husband spoke to the press and one of the first things he said was 'My daughter was not a bum' and he asked if we've come to a place in our country where someone can't speak their mind. By that time we were getting so much mail we couldn't believe it. There were hundreds of letters, pro and con. Some said, Go back to Russia'…or 'Dirty Jew'. Then there were so many people who were so aghast at what had happened and were so kind.

Activities

15. Explain whether you think the mass protests of women's lib, the student movement or the anti-Vietnam War protests had the same sort of impact as the civil rights mass protests.

16. Explain why historians might have difficulties in finding people willing to talk about the attitudes they had in the period 1955–70 towards the civil rights movement, women's lib or Vietnam protests.

17. Explain whether you think a historian should try to understand attitudes that we now find shocking, such as racism, sexism or a willingness to use violence for political aims.

Summary

The historian faces various problems in dealing with evidence and reaching a judgement about the impact of the mass protests in the USA.

- In some cases there are gaps in the evidence which make it difficult to establish what the reactions of ordinary people were toward the protests.

- The evidence may be contradictory in places.

- The situation is further complicated by the fact that we find some of the attitudes of the time difficult to understand.

Understanding and analysing representations of history

Learning outcomes

By the end of this topic, you should be able to:

- understand what is meant by representations of history
- understand how historical representations are created
- analyse representations and judge how far they differ from one another.

What are representations?

A representation is a depiction of the past either visually or in words. It is designed to create an image of things in the past – an event, a movement, the role of an individual and so on. Historians create representations when they write about the past. They construct for us a picture of what life was like, why people acted as they did, and what the consequences of events and developments were. Novelists, filmmakers and cartoonists also give us an image of past societies and events. In each case, the way they choose to show their subject creates a representation of it.

Analysing representations

Someone who creates a representation takes some of the same steps you might take when taking a photograph or creating a Facebook entry. You choose what you are taking a photograph of or how to show yourself. Do you want to record an important event? And do you want to show it as happy or solemn? Do you want to show the beauty of a particular place? To get the effect you want, you choose which things to focus on. Sometimes you decide to leave things out. In this way, you make decisions about how to portray the scene or the event.

When you analyse a representation you should look at each part separately and think about how it affects the overall image. From the details, you can infer (work out) what impression the artist or author is trying to give.

A modern example of a representation

Let's first take a modern example and use the same skills needed to analyse a historical representation. Study Source A.

Source A: An illustration from the website of the British Tourist board, 2009. It shows a scene on the east coast of England.

| Inclusion of the boat and the windmill. | Blue sky: would the photograph have been taken on a rainy day? | Uncrowded scene: no objects in the centre of the picture. | Happy-looking young couple: do people look happy all the time? Why has the photographer not shown just one person alone? |

Note the details the photographer has chosen to include. Why have these details been included? What messages are they designed to give? Can you suggest anything which may have been deliberately left out? What do you think is the purpose of the representation in Source A?

Now study Source B. It is a photograph taken in the middle of an August morning. It shows a part of the coast near to the place shown in Source A. The building in the background is a nuclear power station.

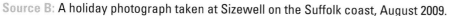

Source B: A holiday photograph taken at Sizewell on the Suffolk coast, August 2009.

What parts of Source A are supported by details in Source B? Would you use Source B to advertise holidays on the Suffolk coast? If not, why not? If so, what parts of the photograph would you select? Source A is not inaccurate, but Source B helps to show us that Source A is not a complete representation.

Source A is one view and when we analyse it, we can infer the message and purpose of this representation from the choices the photographer has made. Source A is designed to portray the coast as attractive and uncrowded, a place to enjoy walks and be happy. Its purpose is to encourage people to take holidays in the area.

Activities

1. Describe the representation of the east coast of England given in Source A. Use details from Source A. You could begin 'Source A is a representation of the East Coast. It is designed to portray it as…We can tell this because…'

2. Try to use most of the following words and phrases in your description. You can use them in any order:
   - selected
   - chosen to
   - omitted
   - deliberately
   - highlighted
   - included
   - incomplete.

   You can also use details from Source B if you wish.

A case study in historical representations: media and protest

Analysing visual representations

In Part B of your controlled assessment, you need to compare and evaluate two or three representations. As you have seen, a representation is a deliberate attempt to create an overall impression. An image has been chosen or created to convey a particular message and you will need to be able to identify and analyse the message in each representation.

On pages 60–61 you saw that the decision to include or leave out details can alter the impression given in a source. However, the treatment of details within a source is also important, for example, what is emphasised or what is presented negatively?

Source C: A plaque marking the site of the F.W. Woolworth store in Greensboro where the 1960 sit-ins began. The top of the plaque says 'Birthplace of the civil rights movement. Four students at North Carolina A & T State University conducted the first lunch counter sit-in on February 1, 1960 at the Woolworth Store.'

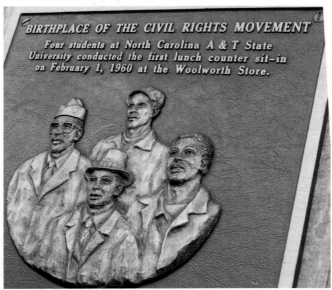

Analysing cartoons

Remember that the key point about representations is that they are created with the intention of giving a particular impression. Cartoons are often used to make a political point in a humorous way. For example, the cartoon in Source D about President Kennedy is saying that he is not in control of events to do with the civil rights movement.

3. Study Source C. Explain which of the following words could be used to describe the people shown on the plaque:
   - angry
   - dignified
   - afraid
   - determined
   - peaceful.
4. What do you think is meant by the phrase on the plaque about 'taking a seat'?
5. What impression of the sit-in is created by the claim that the plaque marks the site of the 'birthplace of the civil rights movement'?

Source D: A cartoon that was printed in a Chicago newspaper, 5 June 1963.

The saddle blanket has 'Civil Rights' written on it.

The reins have broken, there is no way to steer or control the horse.

Kennedy is being bounced out of the saddle and only staying on the horse by clinging to its neck.

The horse is galloping at speed.

The caption says 'Runaway'.

As you can see, the details included in Source D have been carefully selected to make the point that the movement is going faster than the president wants.

Source E: A cartoon by Tom Toles in 2005, when Rosa Parks died.

Analysing the use of photographs

Source F: A photograph of Elizabeth Eckford being turned away from Central High School in Little Rock by the National Guard. The photograph on page 8 shows a crowd taunting her as she walks away afterwards.

When books are covering the civil rights movement, they often choose the picture of the police dogs being used in Birmingham (see Source B on page 16) to illustrate the text because it seems to sum up the brutal tactics of the police and the non-violence of the protesters. The author decides to include this image because it portrays the two sides of the issue. However, this is misleading because using the photograph suggests that this was a typical tactic of the authorities, whereas in fact, most people were shocked and felt that the heavy-handed action was extreme.

Activities 63

6. Study Source D. Is the civil rights movement being shown in a positive or negative way here? Explain how the details within the picture create that impression.

7. Study Source E and explain:
   - what message is being given about Rosa Parks
   - how the impression is being created.

8. Source F is one of a number of photographs taken by Will Counts at Little Rock High School in 1957. Explain whether this photograph would be a good choice to include in a textbook or article about racial discrimination and segregation.

9. Now turn to page 8, where another of Will Counts' photographs is shown. Why do you think that photograph is used in so many books about the civil rights movement instead of Source F?

Jane Shuter makes a similar point in her book *A Divided Union? The USA 1945–70*. She includes Source G in the section about anti-Vietnam War protests. It was taken at Kent State University where a student was shot dead during the protest and it is often used to convey a contrast between the peaceful tactics of student sit-ins and rallies, and the authorities' readiness to use violence.

Source G: A photograph of Jeffrey Miller, one of the dead students at the Kent State anti-Vietnam War protest in 1970.

In her caption, Shuter says 'The girl kneeling beside him is Mary Ann Vecchio. She was not a student but a fourteen-year-old who had run away from Miami. She did not know Miller' (the dead student). Shuter's comment tells us that the person whose shock and grief are at the centre of the photograph was not personally connected to the dead student and was possibly even not part of the student protest.

Activities

10. Analyse Source G. Explain how the focus on three people within this photograph creates a stronger impression than a wider photograph would have given.

11. How do you think the information Shuter included about Mary Ann Vecchio affects the way the photograph can be used to represent the student protest at Kent State University?

Analysing written representations

Written views also create an image through the choice of words, the selection and omission of details and the organisation of the material. Let's look at a couple of examples.

Source H: From the History of Marches and Mass Actions website.

'Many of our earliest activists were women who felt squeezed out of leadership in [the protest] movements, and were drawn to possibilities for them in the women's movement,' says [Patricia] Ireland [former President of NOW].

In perhaps the first picket ever by NOW members, activists in August 1967 dressed in vintage clothing to protest the old-fashioned policies of *The New York Times*, which… segregated [the employment] ads by gender. In December of the same year, NOW held its first national day of demonstrations in five cities, targeting the Equal Employment Opportunity Commission [which had issued] guidelines approving of the ads…

On August 26, 1970, on the 50th anniversary of women's suffrage [in America], NOW activists organized a 'Women's Strike for Equality'.

Approximately 50,000 women marched in New York and another 100,000 women participated in demonstrations and rallies in 90 cities, 42 states.

Context for Source H

- By 1970, 43% of women in the USA went out to work but only 14% of them were managers. 44% of men earned over $25,000 a year but only 9% of women did.

- The Equal Rights Amendment Act was passed in 1972 by the federal government. However, it also needed to be accepted by the individual states – only 35 states accepted the amendment, so this did not become law.

Activities

12. Study Source H. How does Patricia Ireland create the impression that many early leaders of NOW were unhappy at the way they had been treated in other protest movements?

13. How does the article create the impression that NOW had a great deal of support and its protests would have had an important impact on women's employment?

14. Study the context box. How does this additional information affect your view of the representation of NOW that is given in Source H?

15. Source H is only an extract from an article. To see the whole article, go to www.pearsonhotlinks.com, insert the express code 6459P and then click on 'History of Marches and Mass Actions'. Then read the whole article and explain whether this seems to be an accurate representation of women's protests.

Source I: From *Ain't I a Beauty Queen? Black Women, Beauty and the Politics of Race* by Maxine Leeds Craig (2002).

The Women's Liberation protest captured the attention if not the sympathies of the national media. The image of unruly women mocking symbols of American beauty was broadcast widely by the media…

The press [incorrectly] reported that bras had been burned at the protest, creating the 'bra-burner' image that, for years, allowed critics to [dismiss women's libbers as fanatics]…

Several blocks away, at the Ritz Carlton Hotel, the…NAACP staged the first Miss Black America pageant as a 'positive protest' against the exclusion of black women from the Miss America title…Robin Morgan, who would later emerge as a leader of the women's movement, [commented] on the NAACP protest[.] Morgan said, 'We deplore Miss Black America as much as Miss White America but we understand the black issue involved'.

Written representations can be produced at the time or later, but once again, the author is offering their own interpretation of events. They have decided what to include, what to leave out, what to emphasise and so on, and they will also be influenced by their own views on issues about, for example, racial discrimination, or the use of violence in a protest. All these choices and influences will affect the final representation and that is why written representations, including ones from historians, will often differ from each other.

Creating a representation

The range of sources consulted

The choice of sources to be used as evidence

Overall message contained in the written representation

Decisions about the organisation and presentation of information in their representation

The author's ideas about discrimination or the use of violence

Activities

16. How does Maxine Leeds Craig in Source I suggest that the women's lib protest had a very limited impact on people's attitudes?

17. Why do you think many books on this period mention the protest against the beauty contest (and often include a photograph) but very few mention the NAACP protest that the beauty contest was racist?

Comparing representations

The controlled assessment Part B (i) task will ask you to compare two representations. Make sure you have a clear understanding that an analysis of the differences between two representations should not simply be a list of what is and isn't included in each representation. Your analysis should look at the content of each representation but also the overall attitude or impression it creates.

In fact, you have to decide how different the representations are, so you then need to weigh up the similarities and differences, and reach an overall judgement on the nature and extent of the differences.

Activities

18. Copy and complete the chart below to compare Sources H and I as representations of the impact of women's protests.

	Source H	Source I
Details of tactics included in the source	*Women used clothes to symbolise their protest.* *Women went on strike.* *Marches and rallies organised in a number of cities.*	
Details from source of effect/ impact of protest		*Publicity given but not sympathy.* *Media reports of bra burning created a bad impression.*
Author's use of language, selection, omission and emphasis of details to create an overall impression	*Language is very factual.* *Precise figures used to show how widespread the protests were.* *Nothing included about people's reactions.*	

19. Once you have filled in the details for each source, colour code each point using green to show similarities and red to show differences.

20. Write a paragraph explaining whether the differences between these sources are mainly about specific facts and details, or an overall difference in attitude about the impact of these protests.

Summary

- Representations are created to give an impression of an aspect of the past.

- The impression is created by what is included, and by the way details are drawn or by the words used.

- Historians' interpretations are also representations of the past. They sometimes differ because historians use different sources or have different approaches to the topic.

Evaluating representations

When you are evaluating a representation, you are deciding how good it is. When you evaluate anything in everyday life – what clothes to buy, for example – you use criteria. Does it fit? Is it in fashion? Is it too expensive? Is the colour right for me? You also make some criteria more important than others. If something doesn't fit, you won't buy it, even if the colour is right!

You will also use criteria when you weigh up representations of history. But let's work on an everyday example first, and then you can apply your skills to evaluating historical representations.

Activities

1. Identify three criteria you use when you decide what to eat.

2. With a partner pick a film or TV drama you have both seen.

   a. Choose three criteria by which to evaluate it, for example 'funny' or 'action-packed'.

   b. Give it a rating of 1–3 against each of the criteria, and discuss your rating with your partner. You do not need to agree, but you should each be able to back up the rating you give. Refer specifically to the film or drama.

   c. Give the film or drama an overall star rating of 1–5. Make a display to explain your overall evaluation to your class, making sure you refer to the criteria you have used. Was one criterion so important that it had the most influence on your overall rating?

Using criteria to evaluate representations of history

There are many different kinds of representation. You could be judging between an extract from a history book or a cartoon or a work of historical fiction or a film portrayal of an event in the past. Apply criteria to each of them to make your judgement. But remember, in order to weigh up a historical representation you must first have good knowledge of the issue which is represented.

Using your knowledge, you can apply these tests to a representation:

- Is it **accurate**? Test the representation against what you know. Is it correct?

- Is it **complete**? Does your knowledge suggest important aspects are missing?

- Is it **objective**? Analyse the representation to see whether it is fair or unbalanced in its treatment. Here you could also think about the purpose of the author or artist.

You are now going to evaluate Source A on page 68. It is a representation of an individual civil rights protest and the reaction towards it from the authorities. First study the context box. Then consider individual details within the source. For example, does the photograph create the impression that the marchers were a respectable and orderly group or a mob? Are the troopers waiting patiently, angrily, or anxiously? What does the term 'face-off' suggest about the attitudes of, and the relationship between, the protestors and authorities? Can you infer from the caption whether the magazine disapproves of the use of violence by the authorities?

You will also need a wider knowledge of the events in Selma, the context of civil rights protests and the tensions in society in order to decide whether this accurately and fairly shows the tactics used by the civil rights movement and the reaction of the authorities at Selma.

Activities

3. Copy and complete the following chart, evaluating the value of Source A on page 68, as a representation of the impact of the Selma march.

	How accurate?	How complete?	How objective?
Source A			

4. When you have evaluated Source A using these three different criteria, explain what overall judgement you have reached.

Source A: The cover of *Life* magazine from March 1965. The caption says 'Civil rights face-off at Selma. The Savage Season Begins. Alabama troopers await marching negroes at Selma'.

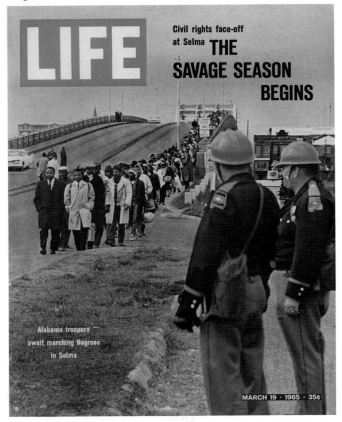

Context for Source A

'Face-off' is a phrase used to describe two opponents staring at each other as they get ready to fight. A face-off is often an attempt to intimidate the enemy so that they back down.

The Selma campaign in 1965 was part of an ongoing campaign to increase the number of black people registered to vote (see page 18). However, Martin Luther King also expected the local sheriff to respond with violence – which could gain the protestors a great deal of sympathy as it had done at Birmingham (see page 16). This was therefore a very tense moment for both the protestors and the authorities as both sides were aware of the power of the media and neither wanted to back down.

When you think about how complete the representation is, remember that no individual source can possibly show all aspects of a situation. Source A doesn't tell you about events before the march or how the public reacted afterwards, but it is not intended to – it is a representation of a single event.

So, another aspect to consider is the purpose behind the representation. Source A was a magazine cover. It was intended to offer a comment on society and events at the time and uses this image to symbolise the conflict between civil rights protestors and the authorities.

Evaluating cartoons

Context for Source B

In his 'I have a dream' speech at the March on Washington in August 1963 (see page 16), Martin Luther King spoke about the American Declaration of Independence which says that all men are created equal. He said that black Americans were not yet treated as being equal to white Americans but he had a dream that it would happen at some point and both sides would live together peacefully.

Source B: A cartoon about the election of Barack Obama in 2008 as the first black president of the United States.

The cartoonist in Source B clearly expects his audience to understand the reference to King's speech (see the context box). He is suggesting that Obama's election is the fulfilment of the civil rights protests in the 1960s and that King's dream of equality has finally been achieved.

Activity

5. Repeat the steps you worked through in Activities 3 and 4, applying them to Source B and evaluating it as a representation of the impact of Martin Luther King's role in the civil rights movement.

Evaluating the use of photographs in representations

Source C: This photograph, taken at the protest in 1968 outside the Miss America beauty pageant in Atlantic City, shows a bra being dropped into a trash can. It is often used as an example of the women's lib protests.

Context for Source C

Nell Greenfieldboyce on the American NPR radio station explained how women protesting at the 1968 Miss America beauty pageant dumped items like bras, pots and pans, and copies of Playboy magazine into a big rubbish bin outside the contest.

The women at this protest had wanted to set fire to the trash can containing all the symbols of their oppression but they were not allowed to do this on the street. However, the actions of anti-war protestors, burning their draft cards, seems to have led to the idea that women burned their bras to symbolise their freedom and to show that they would not live their lives according to men's ideas of beauty and femininity. Even though bra-burning did not happen, it is sometimes wrongly assumed that this is what the photograph shows.

Activities

6. Analyse Source C. What aspects of this photograph look deliberately posed?

7. Why do you think many writers choose to include the photograph in Source C when they write about the women's movement?

Activity

8. How can you test the accuracy of representations like cartoons in Source B and the photograph in Source C which are often intended to represent attitudes rather than be an accurate record of events?

Evaluating written representations

Written representations should be evaluated in the same way as an image. Consider first whether the information is accurate. Then think about whether it is complete. Don't get involved in listing all the details it doesn't mention – remember, a single representation couldn't cover all aspects of mass protests, so the author will have selected certain details to symbolise a wider range of events and it is this act of selection that you need to consider. Finally, think about whether the representation is objective and presents a balanced view.

Source D: An extract taken from the website of the NBC American news channel. John Lewis, who is quoted here, was a leading civil rights activist and badly beaten during the 'Bloody Sunday' event; he is now a member of Congress.

More than 40 years ago, in an attack that became known as Bloody Sunday, Alabama state troopers beat civil rights activists marching for voting rights… That infamous day, and later marches, put the issue before the nation and pushed Congress to act.

CBS and NBC, which had recently expanded news programs to a half-hour, both broadcast the march and its aftermath; CBS produced a special report on the event, and ABC interrupted a prime-time movie to air footage of the assault.

'The nation saw what had happened,' Lewis said. 'People couldn't stand it. They saw the photographs in the newspapers and magazines. They saw the video on television. There was a sense of righteous indignation.'

Context for Source D

'Bloody Sunday' in Alabama was the name given to the police attack on protestors in the first march to Selma in 1965.

Source D suggests that the way the media showed the authorities dealing with the protestors had a significant influence on public attitudes, leading to changes in the law. Source E also portrays the role of the media as important in bringing about change. However, while Source D emphasises the way the media covered events (a 'special report', 'interrupted a prime-time movie') and the effect on the public of seeing this violence, Source E focuses on the way that seeing the violence pushed Robert Kennedy, as Attorney General, to take action.

Source E: From a civil rights website.

> The ordeals of Freedom Riders were widely publicised throughout the world and generated significant support for the cause of racial desegregation in the South. The spectacle of young student protestors being beaten viciously by white mobs convinced Attorney General Robert Kennedy that greater action on behalf of desegregation activists was needed. As a result of his urging, the Interstate Commerce Commission finally banned racial segregation on interstate bus transportation on September 22, 1961.

This is a very different emphasis – did the push for change come from the public or from individuals in government? If Sources D and E were set for the controlled assessment you would have discussed this difference in question B(i) (see page 66), but in question B(ii) of the controlled assessment you would then need to consider which of three sources gives the best representation of the impact of mass protest. You would also need to make clear what criteria you used to reach your judgement.

Activities

9. Repeat the steps you carried out in Activities 3 and 4 when you evaluated Sources A and B, applying them to Sources D and E.

10. Using your work for Activity 9, explain whether D or E gives the better representation of the impact of civil rights protests.

11. Use the sources in this section to create a chart or ideas map showing the strengths and weaknesses of these visual and written representations.

Evaluating representations created by historians

Historians aim to give you their view of past events. They have researched the topic and the details in their writings are likely to be accurate. But question B(ii) of your controlled assessment is all about which representation is the 'best' one so you need to think carefully about what it is that you want to find out.

Look back at the ideas map on page 65 showing the factors influencing the creation of a written representation. The historian is presenting a judgement based on factual research but it is still a personal interpretation of what is important. You need to take this into account when you decide which representation is 'best' for your enquiry.

ResultsPlus
Top Tip

Remember, two people can come to different judgements about which representation is better and still get the same marks. The important thing is to be able to explain which criteria you have used and to back up your comments using the representations themselves and your own knowledge.

Considering the focus of the representation

An additional point to consider is the focus of the representation.

Is a detailed view of one aspect of mass protests and their impact 'better' than an overview of different aspects fitting together?

One of the big questions to consider when thinking about the impact of mass protests is how far they actually led to change. Our evidence suggests:

- The use of violence by the authorities was heavily publicised.
- Many people were genuinely concerned over civil rights, the Vietnam war and the position of women in society.
- Changes in attitudes were very slow to spread.
- Even when the federal authorities made changes to the law, there was a great deal of resistance in some areas.

But the historian's focus will affect the way they write about their topic:

- A biographer of Martin Luther King might concentrate on events such as the Bus Boycott and Birmingham campaign rather than the Little Rock Campaign or the Freedom Riders. They may portray King as a national leader and emphasise successful aspects of the protests.
- A historian writing about the civil rights movement would include organisations such as CORE, the Black Panthers and leaders such as Malcolm X. They might suggest King's tactics were not very successful and emphasise the slow pace of change.
- A historian focusing on why King was assassinated will emphasise opposition to the civil rights movement.

So when you analyse a representation, use your understanding of the context to check how accurate and complete it is but also look at the title of the book and think about the purpose of the representation. If you are considering the impact of mass protests does that mean the short-term impact (the amount of publicity they received at the time) or the long-term impact (whether the situation actually changed)? With the benefit of hindsight, the historian can look back from a later date and see events in a different perspective. For example, Source F makes it clear that even if the civil rights protests were successful in getting legal and political changes, their impact on attitudes was less clear, and even by the 1990s, society was not fully integrated.

Source F: From *America Divided, the Civil War of the 1960s*, by M. Isserman and M. Kazin, published in 2000.

The landmark civil rights bills, helped to pry open opportunities for millions of African Americans. Since the '60s, the number of black political officials, elected and appointed, skyrocketed...By the mid 1990s young blacks were graduating from high school at the same rate as whites...[and] black graduates enjoyed access to nearly every university in the land...

It was more difficult to tell how much racial attitudes had changed since the '60s...Most people socialized only within their own race and...old fashioned styles of racism continued to fester. Numbers of real-estate agents still steered black tenants away from white neighbourhoods...Fortunately millions of Americans... made friends across the color line, particularly at work, and enjoyed a [multi-racial] popular culture.

Activities

12. Use the steps outlined in Activities 3 and 4 to assess Source F.

13. Sources B and F both give a long-term assessment of what changes happened as a result of the civil rights movement. Does that make them 'better' representations of the impact of mass protest than Source A which only shows the response in 1965?

Summary

- A historian's writing will usually be accurate and objective.
- Criteria must always be used when evaluating representations.
- The criteria could be: the accuracy, comprehensiveness, objectivity, and purpose or focus of the representation.
- Representations must be evaluated in their historical context.

ResultsPlus
Maximise your marks

Part A Carry out a historical enquiry

In this task, you are required to carry out an enquiry; the enquiry focus will be set by Edexcel. The task is worth 20 marks and you should aim to spend about an hour writing it up. The mark scheme below shows how your teacher will mark your work for this task. Remember that in this task you are also assessed on the quality of your written communication: use historical terminology where appropriate, organise the information clearly and coherently, and make sure your spelling, punctuation and grammar are accurate.

Level	Answers at this level…	Marks available
Level 1	Make simple comments. There are few links between them and few details are given. Only one or two sources have been used in the enquiry.	1–5 marks
Level 2	Make statements about the enquiry topic. Information is included that is mostly relevant and accurate, but it is not well organised to focus on the point of the enquiry. A range of sources has been consulted and information taken from them.	6–10 marks
Level 3	Are organised to focus mainly on the point of the enquiry. Accurate and relevant information is given to support the points the student makes. A range of sources has been found and well-chosen material taken from them.	11–15 marks
Level 4	Focus well on the point of the enquiry. A well-supported conclusion is reached, for example about: the nature of change OR whether one factor was more important than the others OR the inter-relationship between two or more of the factors (depending on the enquiry focus). A range of sources appropriate to the enquiry has been identified and material from the sources has been well deployed.	16–20 marks

Let's look at an extract from one response to the following enquiry:

- The importance of the student protest movement 1960–1970

Extract from student's answer

The student protest was based in the universities. These students saw the injustice that was happening in America and they spoke out about it.

Many students were involved in the civil rights movement, especially the SNCC – the Student Non-Violent Coordinating Committee. Nigel Ritchie gives details of this in his book 'The Civil Rights Movement'. The student movement gave the students a chance to work together at university.

In their book 'Pursuing Life and Liberty', Bunce and Gallagher describe how the group Students for a Democratic Society started in 1960 at Michigan University. They explain how the students set out their aims in the Port Huron Statement in 1962, that the government should be trying to use wealth to make life better for everyone rather than concentrating on profit.

Bunce and Gallagher also explain how another group, formed at the University of California in Berkeley and led by Mario Savio, demanded free speech after the university tried to restrict student political actions.

However, the biggest issue of student protest was the Vietnam War. The Spartacus website explains how the decision to increase conscription led to protest among students even though students at university were exempt from the draft.

Shuter's book, 'A Divided Union', also has a section on student protests and describes their tactics. These included sit-ins, strikes, and more violent actions which led to them being arrested. Sometimes the university lecturers agreed with the students and they held teach-ins where they gave lectures and the students occupied the building and refused to leave.

The most famous protest was at Kent State University in Ohio in 1970. Waugh and Wright describe this in their book, 'A Divided Union', and explain how the protest started as a demonstration against Nixon's decision to bomb Cambodia (he did this in order to prevent supplies reaching the Communists in Vietnam). National Guardsmen were called in to disperse the crowd and used tear gas but the students still refused to move, so shots were fired and four were killed.

This episode received great publicity and this shows how important the student protest movement was.

Moderator's comment

This extract indicates that the response would gain a mark in Level 2.

The response describes the development of the student movement but does not explain its importance. Lots of details are provided about the protest movement but the focus is on what the students were protesting about and what happened rather than what effect the protest had.

The student has used textbooks and an internet site to provide information. Material has been selected for relevance and the student has combined notes from different sources. However, the material has not been smoothly integrated and details are taken from each source in turn rather than a well planned comment from the student based on a range of details. The Quality of Written Communication is generally good, the meaning is clear and correct historical terminology is used but the information is not well organised into paragraphs, instead each point is presented separately.

To improve the response, the focus should look more centrally at the precise enquiry: the importance of the student protest movement. The response could show importance by looking at:

- How many people and which social groups were involved.
- What publicity the protests received and the attitudes of both the media and the public.
- How the authorities reacted.

Extract from student's improved answer

The student protest was focused on the universities. These students were educated and able to think for themselves so they saw the injustice that was happening in American society and they were confident enough to speak out about it. They also tended to come from middle-class families and therefore their protests could not be easily ignored because these families usually accepted authority and would not normally oppose the government or police, so they were not 'troublemakers'. Student protests were also serious for the government because increasing wealth and better education opportunities for girls had increased the number of students at university, so although this group was a minority in society, the government could not claim that the protests were unimportant.

The first organisation of students was the group Students for a Democratic Society, started in 1960 at Michigan University. In their book 'Pursuing Life and Liberty', Bunce and Gallagher explain how the students set out their aims in the Port Huron Statement in 1962, suggesting that rather than concentrating on profit, the government should be trying to use wealth to make life better for everyone. This idea was a challenge to the American way of life but at this stage the organisation was still quite small and it had little impact on society or the authorities.

Bunce and Gallagher also explain how another group, formed at the University of California in Berkeley and led by Mario Savio, demanded free speech after the university tried to restrict student political actions. This group had quite a big impact at Berkeley because eventually the college authorities backed down and the students were allowed to campaign on political issues and freedom of speech was restored.

Many students were individually involved in the civil rights movement, especially the SNCC – the Student Non-Violent Coordinating Committee – and the Mississippi Freedom Summer in 1964. Nigel Ritchie gives details of this in his book 'The Civil Rights Movement'. However, the organised student protests of the 1960s did not particularly focus on civil rights and at this stage, the student movement was not co-ordinated.

Instead, the event which caused the student movement to become a big issue was the Vietnam War. The Spartacus website explains how the decision to increase conscription led to protest among students even though students at university were exempt from the draft. The students used a range of tactics such as sit-ins, strikes, and more violent actions which led to them being arrested. Sometimes the university lecturers agreed with the students and they held teach-ins where they gave lectures and the students occupied the building and refused to leave. These are described in Shuter's book 'A Divided Union' but the scale of the protest can be seen more clearly on the website http://www.lib.berkeley.edu/MRC/pacificaviet.html.

ResultsPlus
Maximise your marks

The government could not ignore such large scale protests and it is suggested that the anti-Vietnam War protests were a major reason why Johnson did not stand for re-election as president. It is difficult to tell how influential the student movement was, but there was a great deal of publicity given to students rallies, especially when they were chanting 'Hey, hey, LBJ, how many kids did you kill today?'

Student protests continued to get publicity under Nixon, especially the one at Kent State University in Ohio in 1970. Waugh and Wright describe this in their book 'A Divided Union' and explain how the protest was begun to complain about Nixon's decision to bomb Cambodia in order to prevent supplies reaching the Communists in Vietnam. National Guardsmen were called in to disperse the crowd and used tear gas but the students still refused to move, so shots were fired and four were killed. This was headline news around the world and the publicity this received made the student protests very important.

However, as the USA withdrew from Vietnam, the student movement collapsed. Although there were feminist groups and groups campaigning for racial equality, it was the issue of Vietnam that united them and it was only when they were united that the student movement had a big impact on society or the authorities.

Part B(i) Compare two representations

In this task, you are required to analyse and compare two representations of history.
The task is worth 10 marks and you should aim to spend about 30 minutes writing it up.
The mark scheme below shows how your teacher will mark your work for this task.

Level	Answers at this level...	Marks available
Level 1	Show an understanding of the main features of the two representations and select material from them. The answer is based on descriptions, direct quotations, or paraphrases from one or more of the sources.	1–3 marks
Level 2	Show an understanding of the two representations and select similarities and/or differences of detail from them. At low level 2, there may be only one developed comparison, and other comparisons will be undeveloped or unsupported with material from the sources.	4–7 marks
Level 3	Analyse the sources and identify a range of similarities and/or differences in representation, using precisely selected detail from the two representations to support the explanation. Make a judgement about how much the representations create different views.	8–10 marks

Let's look at an extract from one student's response to the representations below.

- Study Representation C on page 62 and Representation F on page 71. They are both representations of the impact of mass protest on US society in the 1960s. How far do these representations differ? (10 marks)

Extract from student's answer

Representations C and F are both about the way civil rights protests improved the situation of black people. Representation F gives us lots of examples of ways in which black people got better treatment in America and it says this started from the protests of the 1960s. However, Representation F also says that although laws have changed the official situation, people's attitudes took a lot longer to change.

Representation C agrees that the situation of black people in America has improved since the 1960s and picks out the sit-in as a key point. However, Representation C is different because it does not give us any detail about how the situation changed or how much difference this protest made. So overall they differ quite a bit, because Representation F talks about how the situation improved generally while Representation C is just about one key event.

ResultsPlus
Maximise your marks

Moderator comment

In this part of the answer, the student has understood the details in the sources and is comparing them. We can see the language of comparison is used: 'are both about', 'agrees', 'is different because', 'differ quite a bit'.

The student has noted the details which are similar in both sources and also where one author provides details which the other has not included. The student has also noted that there is a different focus in each representation.

There is enough comprehension and comparison for the answer to get into level 2, but the answer concentrates mainly on differences in details in the two sources. To raise the response to the next level, the answer should offer more explanation of the different focus in these two representations. Representation F's focus is on weighing up how much actually changed for black people, showing that people's attitudes did not change as quickly as the laws did. Representation C's focus is on a specific protest and suggests that it was a key event. Representation C suggests that the civil rights protests (and especially the sit-in) were a success whereas Representation F is much more cautious in making a judgement.

Extract from student's improved answer

Representations F and C are both about the way civil rights protests improved the situation of black people. Representation F gives us lots of examples of ways in which black people got better treatment in America and dates it back to the protests of the 1960s. Representation C agrees that the situation of black people in America has improved since the 1960s and picks out the sit-in as a key point.

However, Representation F also talks about the effects of the protests and says that people's attitudes took a long time to change whereas Representation C just talks about one key event. Representation F is giving an overall view whereas Representation C does not give us any detail about how the situation changed or how much difference this protest made. So overall they differ quite a bit in what they actually say.

More importantly, they differ a great deal in attitude. Representation C suggests the civil rights protests were a success story but Representation F shows that using different criteria will give a different answer. The protests were very successful in one way as the laws were changed but if you focus on changing attitudes, the protests achieved far less. Furthermore, Representation F goes on to suggest that the changes in attitude which did eventually occur were because people mixed at work and black and white people enjoyed the same popular culture rather than because of the protests in the 1960s.

Therefore the two representations differ a great deal – not just in how far they think civil rights protests led to change but also in the criteria they use to make a judgement, their approach to the topic and the way that Representation F considers other factors affecting the situation while Representation C does not.

Part B(ii) Analyse and evaluate three representations

In this task, you are required to analyse and evaluate three representations of history. The task is worth 20 marks and you should aim to spend about an hour writing it up. The mark scheme below shows how your teacher will mark your work for this task. Remember that in this task you are also assessed on the quality of your written communication. You should use the correct historical terminology, organise the information clearly and coherently, and make sure your spelling, punctuation and grammar are accurate.

Level	Answers at this level…	Marks available
Level 1	Show an understanding of the main features of the sources and select material. Simple judgements are made about the representation, and a limited amount of accurate information about the period is given. The material is mostly generalised, and links to the representation are not explicit.	1–5 marks
Level 2	Show an understanding of the main features of the three sources and select key features of the representations from them. Judgement is made about the best representation and there is detailed and accurate material about the period, but with little linkage between description and judgement. Judgements may relate to the accuracy or comprehensiveness of the representation.	6–10 marks
Level 3	Analyse the three sources and show some of the ways in which the past situation has been represented. Detail from the sources is used to support the analysis. There is a critical evaluation of the representation based on well selected information about the period and at least two clear criteria are applied, for example, the author's purpose or objectivity, or the accuracy and comprehensiveness of the representation.	11–15 marks
Level 4	Analyse the three sources to show the way in which the past situation has been represented. Precisely selected detail from the sources is used to support the analysis. There is a critical evaluation of the representation based on precisely selected information about the period and applying at least three criteria, for example the author's purposes or objectivity, or the comprehensiveness and/or accuracy of the representation, to all three sources.	16–20 marks

Let's look at an extract from one student's response to the representations below.

- Study Representations C and F again and Representation G, below. Choose the one which you think is the best representation of the effect of mass protest in changing US society. Explain your choice. (20 marks)

Representation G

From *And the Crooked Places Made Straight, the struggle for social change in the 1960s*, by David Chalmers, 1991.

> The young dissenters had tried non-violence, and it had not worked. They had tried violence and that had not worked either…Black radical leaders had been killed by their rivals or the police, or were in exile abroad. The radical student Left had failed in the streets…Malcolm X, [and] Martin Luther King Jr….had been murdered…Whatever the outrage and anguish produced by the war, the 1968 Chicago riots…and the shootings at Kent State and Jackson State, at least a substantial portion of the American people thought the students had gotten what was coming to them.

ResultsPlus
Maximise your marks

Extract from student's response

I think Representation C is useful because it tells us that non-violent protest did achieve some things and it tells us about the moral aspect of these protests. This is something that I know Martin Luther King emphasised, so it fits in with my own knowledge and I can tell it's accurate.

Representation G is also useful because it tells us that mass protests actually had little effect on events in America. In fact, Representation G stresses the failure of these protests and suggests that the violent protests actually lost public support. But it doesn't provide very many details to back up its comments and it doesn't mention the changes in law to stop segregation so this is not very complete or accurate.

However, I think Representation F is the best. It gives us accurate information about the progress in civil rights but also tells us that attitudes were much slower to change. This is very comprehensive because it is giving us a long term view and reaches different judgements based on different criteria, which means it is covering all aspects of the issue.

Moderator comment

The student has commented on all three representations and shown how the detail within each representation is useful. There has also been an attempt to use criteria to evaluate the representations, but none of the comments are developed very far. The student uses the criteria of accuracy and comprehensiveness but uses only a limited amount of own knowledge to test this accuracy and comprehensiveness. To improve the answer, the student should make more use of contextual knowledge and analyse the representations more fully, identifying specific things that are inaccurate or left out.

The student could also look at the focus of the representations – Representations F and C are both about civil rights protests whereas Representation G looks at student anti-Vietnam War protests within a wider context. Another good point to discuss would be how far the nature and purpose of the representations affected their value.

To reach the highest level the student must make use of at least three criteria to rate each representation, but this answer also needs to make more use of contextual knowledge to support the comments made.

ResultsPlus
Maximise your marks

Extract from improved student response

I think Representation C is useful because it is an example of a non-violent protest and Martin Luther King used this tactic in protests such as....Publicity for these protests would show that the black protestors were not doing anything that was illegal for a white person. So the emphasis in the plaque about standing up for what is right is a good representation of the non-violent tactics. It also suggests that the sit-in tactic was successful, which is true because stores did change their policy about lunch counters but water fountains, toilets and interstate buses remained segregated.

So it is a useful representation of one type of tactic but it is not entirely accurate and it is not comprehensive. We should also consider the purpose of the plaque. It was erected to commemorate this specific event. However, the claim that this event was the birthplace of the civil rights movement is exaggerated. It ignores the fact that there were previous campaigns such as...

Representation G tells us that mass protests actually had little effect on events in America. In fact, Representation G portrays the whole protest movement as a failure and suggests that they lacked public support. But this doesn't provide very many details to back up its comments and it doesn't mention that there were changes in law to stop segregation or the way that protests put pressure on the government to withdraw from Vietnam....However, the fact that Representation G refers to both non-violent and violent protests, civil rights and Vietnam is better than Representations F and C which give a more limited view...

However, I think Representation F is the best. It gives us accurate information about the progress in civil rights but also tells us that attitudes were much slower to change. This is very comprehensive because it is written from a different perspective, using hindsight and giving us a long term view. It is also reaching different judgements based on different criteria, which means it is covering all aspects of the issue. It needs to be backed up by more detail but from my own knowledge I can show that the comments are accurate...

The author also seems to be quite objective, giving a balanced view of achievements but also showing failures and the role of other factors...

Overall Representation F is accurate, and more objective and comprehensive than Representation C. Its focus on how much things actually changed and whether that was the result of mass protests also makes it better than Representation G, even though Representation G covers a wider context.

Glossary

Assassination: murder of an individual, often used to affect the political situation.

Black nationalism: the belief that black people should create a black society, independent from white society.

Black Power: movements that aimed to get more power for black people, to fight against the oppression of black people and to help create a strong black identity.

Civil rights: the rights that citizens of a country have by law.

CORE: the Congress of Racial Equality. It began in 1942.

Deep South: the states at the Southern edge of the USA: Louisiana, Alabama, Georgia, Mississippi and South Carolina in particular. These states had been highly dependent on black slave labour for their plantation agriculture before the Civil War.

Direct action: doing something directly to try to make changes, e.g. demonstrations, boycotts, sit-ins. Indirect action would include using your vote to change a situation you don't like.

Draft (the): the system by which young men between the ages of 18 and 25 were selected to serve in the US army.

Federal: the United States is a collection of different states all bound together into a federation, with a federal government and federal laws.

Freedom Riders: a federal law meant interstate buses should not be segregated. Civil rights protestors, known as Freedom Riders, rode on these buses into segregated states to show that the law was often not being obeyed.

Integration: the opposite of segregation but also meaning black Americans having the same opportunities as white Americans, not just the right to access the same services.

Ku Klux Klan: a racist white group.

Mass protest: a protest that involves lots of people, e.g. marches, petitions, boycotts.

NAACP: the National Association for the Advancement of Colored People. It began in 1909.

Nation of Islam: a religious organisation that began in 1930 with the aim of improving life for black Americans. It borrows ideas from the Islamic religion but also has some non-Islamic beliefs.

SCLC: the Southern Christian Leadership Conference. It began in 1957.

Segregation: keeping separate.

Segregationists: supporters of the belief that black and white people should have separate services.

Sit-in: a non-violent type of protest in which protestors sit down in an area and refuse to move.

SNCC: the Student Non-Violent Coordinating Committee. It began in 1960.

States' rights: every state in the USA has its own laws. Generally speaking, the federal government only has the powers that have specifically been given it by the US Constitution: everything else is governed by the state. Some Southerners claimed that they had states' rights to oppose federal law on desegregation.

Published by Pearson Education Limited, a company incorporated in England and Wales, having its registered office at Edinburgh Gate, Harlow, Essex, CM20 2JE. Registered company number: 872828

Edexcel is a registered trademark of Edexcel Limited

First published 2010

12 11 10
10 9 8 7 6 5 4 3 2 1

British Library Cataloguing in Publication Data
A catalogue record for this book is available from the British Library

ISBN 978 1 846906 45 9

Designed and typeset by Juice Creative Ltd, Hertfordshire
Original illustrations © Pearson Education Ltd 2010
Printed in Great Britain at Scotprint, Haddington

Acknowledgements
We would like to thank Martin Thornton for his invaluable help in the development of this material.

Picture credits
The publisher would like to thank the following for their kind permission to reproduce their photographs:

(Key: b-bottom; c-centre; l-left; r-right; t-top)

Alamy Images: Jason O. Watson 62; **Corbis**: 8, 13, 17, 37, 42, Geoffrey Clements 26, Library of Congress - digital ve / Science Faction 23, Flip Schulke 31, Flip Schulke 31; **Getty Images**: 26/2, Dan Farrell / NY Daily News Archive 35, The Washington Post / Bernie Boston 38, Buyenlarge 9, David Fenton 22, 40, David Fenton 22, 40, John Filo 64, Carl Iwasaki / TIME & LIFE Images 7, Keystone 20, Joseph Scherschel / Time & Life Pictures 28, Paul Schutzer / Time & Life Pictures 11, Walter Bennett / Time & Life Pictures 11/2, Agence France Presse 2; **The Picture Collection Inc.**: Charles Moore / Black Star Charles Moore / Black Star / Black Star 68; **Angela Leonard**: 61; **Copyright by Bill Mauldin (1963)**: 62/2; **Photolibrary. com**: Rod Edwards / Britain on View 60; **Press Association Images**: 39, 54, 69, Jackson Daily News, Fred Blackwell 57, AP Photo / Bill Hudson 16, White House, Cecil Stoughton 27; The Advertising Archives: Image courtesy of **The Advertising Archives** 59; **Universal Uclick**: Tim Toles / The Washington Post 63/2, Toles 68/2; **Indiana University**: 63; **University of California, Berkeley**: 41

Cover images: Front: Corbis: Flip Schulke, Flip Schulke

All other images © Pearson Education

Text
We are grateful to the following for permission to reproduce copyright material:

Quote on page 9 from President Eisenhower televised address http://128.83.78.2/nl/podcasttext_dde_01.pdf, 24/09/1957; Extract on page 10 from 'Verdict of Alabama Middle District Court in Browder v. Gayle, November 1956', http://www.archives.gov/southeast/education/resources-by-state/images/alabama-judgment.pdf, source: National Archives and Records Administration; Extract on page 22 from 'Black Panther Ten Point Plan', http://www.blackpanther.org/TenPoint.htm, copyright © The Dr. Huey P.Newton Foundation Inc.; Quote on page 29 from President Eisenhower on the Brown decision in May 1954; Extract on page 52 from 'The results of a series of public opinion polls during the 1960s' http://www.historylearningsite.co.uk/black_panthers.htm, reproduced by permission of the History Learning Site; Extract on pages 41, 46-47 from *Democracy's Children*, Scholarly Resources Inc., U.S. (Spann, E.K. 2003) pp.72-73, 86-89 copyright © Rowman & Littlefield Publishing Group Inc.; Extract on page 47 from 'Watts Riots, 40 years Later', *LA Times*, 11/08/2005 (Valerie Reitman and Mitchell Landsberg), http://www.latimes.com/news/local/la-me-watts11aug11,0,4693415,full.story, reproduced by permission of Los Angeles Times; Extract on page 51 from 'Martin Luther King, Jr. Day on the Net - Rosa Parks and the Montgomery Bus Boycott', Holidays on the Net, http://www.holidays.net/mlk/rosa.htm, reproduced with permission; Extract on page 51 from Article about the Black Panthers, *The Socialist Worker*, 2007, www.socialistworker.co.uk, copyright © Socialist Worker; Extract on page 56 from 'The Nobel Prize in Peace 1964, Martin Luther King Jr', http://nobelprize.org/nobel_prizes/peace/laureates/1964/king-bio.html, source: The Nobel Foundation; Extract on page 64 from 'The History of Marches and Mass Actions', http://www.now.org/history/protests.html, Reprinted with permission of National Organization for Women.

Figures
Figure on page 55 from Presidential Job Approval Center, The Gallup Poll 2004: Public Opinion, http://www.gallup.com/poll/124922/Presidential-Approval-Centre.aspx, copyright © 2004 Gallup, Inc. All rights reserved.

In some instances we have been unable to trace the owners of copyright material, and we would appreciate any information that would enable us to do so.

Websites
The websites used in this book were correct and up to date at the time of publication. It is essential for tutors to preview each website before using it in class so as to ensure that the URL is still accurate, relevant and appropriate. We suggest that tutors bookmark useful websites and consider enabling students to access them through the school/college intranet.

Disclaimer
This material has been published on behalf of Edexcel and offers high-quality support for the delivery of Edexcel qualifications. This does not mean that the material is essential to achieve any Edexcel qualification, nor does it mean that it is the only suitable material available to support any Edexcel qualification. Edexcel material will not be used verbatim in setting any Edexcel examination or assessment. Any resource lists produced by Edexcel shall include this and other appropriate resources.

Copies of official specifications for all Edexcel qualifications may be found on the Edexcel website: www.edexcel.com